Framework English

Skills in Fiction

Geoff Reilly and **Wendy Wren**

Series Consultant: **John Jackman**

OXFORD
UNIVERSITY PRESS

Contents

Sherlock Holmes, a gentleman detective, and his associate, Dr Watson are the creation of the author, Sir Arthur Conan Doyle. Succeeding in solving strange and bizarre crimes which baffled the police, Holmes is able to find and piece together clues in an amazing way.

The story so far…

In this adventure, a young lady named Helen Stoner visits Mr Sherlock Holmes to ask for his help as she is in fear of her life. She fills in her background and these are the important points:

> *She lived in India where her father died.*
>
> *Her mother married Dr Roylott, a man of violent temper, returned to England and died eight years ago.*
>
> *Dr Roylott has her mother's money but has to share it with the two girls when they marry.*
>
> *He has an interest in Indian animals and keeps a cheetah and a baboon at his ancestral house of Stoke Moran.*
>
> *Helen has a twin sister who died in a mysterious way two weeks before she was due to be married.*
>
> *The only other people at the house are a band of gypsies whom Dr Roylott allows to camp on his land.*

Helen's story…

'The manor house is, as I have already said, very old and only one wing is now inhabited. The bedrooms on this wing are on the ground floor, the sitting rooms being in the central block of the buildings. Of these bedrooms the first is Dr Roylott's, the second my sister's and the third my own. There is no communication between them, but they all open out into the same corridor. Do I make myself plain?'

'Perfectly so.'

'The windows of the three rooms open out upon the lawn. That fatal night Dr Roylott had gone to his room early, though we knew that he had not retired to rest, for my sister was troubled by the smell of the strong Indian cigars which it was his custom to smoke. She left her room therefore, and came into mine, where she sat for some time chatting about her approaching wedding. At eleven o'clock she rose to leave me, but she paused at the door and looked back.

'"Tell me, Helen," said she, "have you ever heard anyone whistle in the dead of the night?"

'"Never," said I.

'"I suppose you could not possibly whistle, yourself, in your sleep?"

'"Certainly not. But why?"

'"Because during the last few nights I have always, about three in the morning, heard a low, clear whistle. I am a light sleeper, and it has awakened me. I cannot tell where it came from, perhaps from the next room, perhaps from the lawn. I thought I would just ask you whether you had heard it?"

'"No, I have not. It must be those wretched gypsies in the plantation."

'"Very likely. And yet if it were on the lawn, I wonder that you did not hear it also."

'"Ah, but I sleep more heavily than you."

'"Well, it is of no great consequence, at any rate." She smiled back at me, closed the door, and a few moments later I heard her key turn in the lock.'

'Indeed,' said Holmes. 'Was it your custom always to lock yourselves in at night?'

'Always.'

'And why?'

'I think I mentioned to you that the doctor kept a cheetah and a baboon. We had no feeling of security unless our doors were locked.'

'Quite so. Pray proceed with your statement.'

'I could not sleep that night. A vague feeling of impending misfortune impressed me. My sister and I, you will recollect, were twins, and you know how subtle are the links which bind two souls which are so closely allied. It was a wild night. The wind was howling outside, and the rain was beating and splashing against the windows. Suddenly, amid all the hubbub of the gale, there burst forth the wild scream of a terrified woman. I knew that it was my sister's voice. I sprang from my bed, wrapped a shawl round me, and rushed into the corridor. As I opened my door I seemed to hear a low whistle, such as my sister described, and a few moments later a clanging sound, as if a mass of metal had fallen. As I ran down the passage, my sister's door was unlocked, and revolved slowly upon its hinges. I stared at it horror-stricken, not knowing what was about to issue from it. By the light of the corridor lamp I saw my sister appear at the opening, her face blanched with terror, her hands groping for help, her whole figure swaying to and fro like that of a drunkard. I ran to her and threw my arms around her, but at that moment her knees seemed to give way and she fell to the ground. She withered as one who is in terrible pain, and her limbs were dreadfully convulsed. At first I thought she had not recognised me, but as I bent over her she suddenly shrieked out in a voice which I shall never forget, "Oh, my God! Helen! It was the band! The speckled band!" There was something else she would fain have said, and she stabbed with her finger into the air in the direction of the doctor's room, but a fresh convulsion seized her and choked her words ... Such was the dreadful end of my beloved sister ...'

'And what conclusion did the coroner come to?'

'He investigated the case with great care, for Dr Roylott's conduct had long been notorious in the country, but he was unable to find any satisfactory cause of death. My evidence showed that the door had been fastened upon the inner side, and the windows were blocked by old-fashioned shutters with broad iron bars, which were secured every night. The walls were carefully sounded, and were shown to be quite solid all round, and the flooring was also thoroughly examined, with the same result. The chimney is wide, but is barred up by four large staples. It is certain, therefore, that my sister was quite alone when she met her end. Besides, there were no marks of any violence upon her.'

Sir Arthur Conan Doyle

TEXT LEVEL WORK

Comprehension

A 1 Where were the bedrooms in the inhabited wing of the manor house?

2 How did Helen and her sister know that on '*that fatal night*' Dr Roylott had not '*retired to rest*'?

3 What did Helen's sister tell her she had heard '*during the last three nights*'?

4 For what reason did Helen and her sister lock their doors at night?

5 What conclusion did the coroner come to about the cause of the girl's death?

B 1 Explain the following in your own words:

   a '*Do I make myself plain?*'
   b '*horror-stricken*'
   c '*The walls were carefully sounded.*'

2 Explain why Helen had '*A vague feeling of impending misfortune*'.

3 What impression do you get of the relationship between Helen and her sister? Quote from the passage to support your answer.

4 Do you think the gypsies had anything to do with the girl's death? Why? Why not?

C 1 Through Helen, the writer gives us a very detailed account of what had happened. Find and copy two examples of:

   a the physical description of the house
   b the physical description of the dying girl after Helen heard her scream.

2 What do you think was the writer's intention in giving the reader such a detailed account of what had happened?

WORD LEVEL WORK

Vocabulary

Dictionary and contextual work

Use a dictionary and the context of the passage to explain the meaning of the following words:

1 associate	4 consequence	7 impending	10 convulsed
2 ancestral	5 custom	8 issue	11 fain
3 retired	6 proceed	9 blanched	12 notorious

Spelling

Double 'p'

Key words: **app**roaching   su**pp**ose   **app**ear

1 Use these key words in sentences of your own.

2 Learn these important double 'p' words:

   disa**pp**ear   disa**pp**oint   ha**pp**ened   **app**aratus   **app**lause
   approximately   **app**rove

SENTENCE LEVEL WORK

Grammar and punctuation

Nouns – common and proper

> Remember: a *noun* is a word that names something.
> There are different types of noun:
> - *common nouns* name kinds of things. They refer to something that is a member of a set of similar things, eg
>   A detective is one of a set of people who investigate things.
> - *proper nouns* are the names of specific people, geographical places, days of the week, months, trade names, titles etc, eg
>   Helen, Dr Roylott.

A Copy and complete the table to show which type of noun each word is.

Noun	Common	Proper
India		
cheetah		
Stoke Moran		
baboon		
wing		
Holmes		
gypsies		
God		
band		
Sir Arthur Conan Doyle		

B Write a sentence of your own for each of the nouns in the table.

TEXT LEVEL WORK

Writing

Recounts in stories

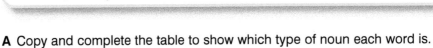

> At some point in many detective stories, a witness to the crime, the perpetrator of the crime or a policeman involved in the investigation recounts in detail what they saw, did or found out.
>
> In *The Speckled Band*, Helen recounts in great detail the last time she saw her sister alive and what happened up to the time of her death.
>
> This type of detailed recount:
> - ensures the reader knows as much as the detective at any time
> - can plant clues for the reader to follow
> - can throw the reader off the scent by including 'red herrings'.

Language features

First person account

Usually the character with information relates it to the reader directly through conversation with another character. In *The Speckled Band*, Helen tells Sherlock Holmes exactly what she knows about the mysterious circumstances of her sister's death. For example:

> '*I could not sleep that night.*'
> '*As I opened the door ...*'
> '*I ran to her ...*'.

Detailed description

It is obviously very important for the detective and the reader to know the precise details of where the crime took place ie the location, eg

- Was the scene of the crime easily accessible to lots of people?
- Was there somewhere the murderer could hide?
- Was it easy for the murderer to make his escape?

The reader can picture the location through the details which Helen gives to Sherlock Holmes, eg

> '*The bedrooms on this wing are on the ground floor ...*'
> '*... they all open out into the same corridor*'.

Clues and red herrings

Helen's detailed account sets the scene for Sherlock Holmes and the reader. Included in it are genuine clues that will help the detective solve the mystery and also red herrings which could lead him to investigate things which are of no importance. But – which are the clues and which are the red herrings?

- the whistle in the dead of night?
- the gypsies camped in the plantation?
- the cheetah and the baboon?
- the clanging sound?

Atmosphere

Often in detective stories the evil crime is reflected in the time and the weather conditions to add to the horror, eg

> '*The manor house is, as I have said, very old ...*'

> '*It was a wild night. The wind was howling outside, and the rain was beating and splashing against the window. Suddenly, amid all the hubbub of the gale ...*'.

Writing assignment

Imagine that you are a guest at a large house for the weekend. There are ten other people staying. You and several others are disturbed in the night and, when you investigate, find the murdered body of Patricia Plumstaff in the library. Sherlock Holmes is called in and interviews you one at a time. What can you tell him?

Write an account of your movements from the time you said goodnight to the other guests and retired to bed until you found the body in the library.

Got the car ready?...

In The Silent World of Nicholas Quinn, *Sergeant Lewis has informed Chief Inspector Morse by phone that a body has been found. They meet in the police station and Lewis fills in the information so far ...*

Morse sat back in his black-leather armchair and beamed at Lewis. 'Well? What have you got to tell me?'

'Chap called Quinn, sir. Lives on the ground floor of a semi-detached in Pinewood Close. He's been dead for a good while by the look of him. Poisoned, I shouldn't wonder. He works' ('worked', muttered Morse) 'at the Foreign Examinations Syndicate down the Woodstock Road somewhere; and one of his colleagues got worried about him and came out and found him. I got the call about a quarter to ten, and I went along straightaway with Dickson and had a quick look round. I left him there, and came back to call you.'

'Well, here I am, Lewis. What do you want me to do?'

'Knowing you, sir, I thought you might want me to arrest the chap who found him.'

Morse grinned. 'Is he here?'

'In the Interview Room. I've got a rough statement from him, but it'll need a bit of brushing up before he signs it. You'll want to see him, I suppose?'

'Yes, but that can wait. Got the car ready?'

'Waiting outside, sir.'

'You've not called the path. boys in yet, I hope?'

'No. I thought I ought to wait for you.'

'Good. Go and get your statement tarted up and I'll see you outside in ten minutes or so.'

Morse made two phone calls, combed his hair again, and felt inordinately happy ...

... The front door of No 1 Pinewood Close opened on to a narrow hallway, with a row of clothes pegs at the foot of the staircase which climbed the wall to the left. Morse stood inside and pointed to the door immediately to his right. 'This the one?'

'Next one, sir.'

The door was closed and Morse took out his pen and depressed the handle carefully. 'I hope you haven't left your prints all over the place, Lewis?'

'I opened it in the same way as you, sir.'

Inside the room the electric light was still turned on; the dull-orange curtains were drawn; the gas fire was burning low; and lying in a foetal posture on the carpet was the body of a young man. The fire was flanked by two old, but comfortable looking armchairs; and beside the one to the right, on a low French-polished coffee-table, stood a bottle of dry sherry, almost full, and a cheap-looking sherry glass, almost empty. Morse bent forward and sniffed the pale, clear liquid. 'Did you know, Lewis, that about eighteen per cent of men and about four per cent of women can't smell cyanide?'

'It is poison, then?'

'Smells like it. Peach blossom, bitter almonds – take your pick.'

The dead man's face was turned towards them, away from the fire, and Morse knelt down and looked at it. A small quantity of dry froth crusted the twisted mouth, and the bearded jaw was tightly clenched in death; the pupils of the open eyes appeared widely dilated, and the skin of the face was a morbid, blotchy blue. 'All the classic symptoms,

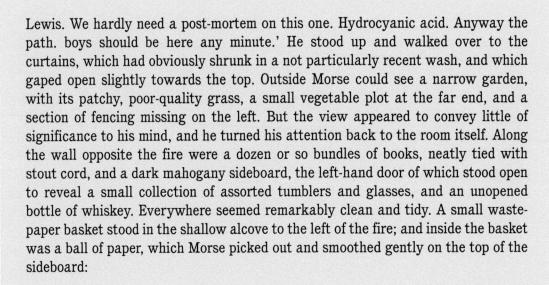

Lewis. We hardly need a post-mortem on this one. Hydrocyanic acid. Anyway the path. boys should be here any minute.' He stood up and walked over to the curtains, which had obviously shrunk in a not particularly recent wash, and which gaped open slightly towards the top. Outside Morse could see a narrow garden, with its patchy, poor-quality grass, a small vegetable plot at the far end, and a section of fencing missing on the left. But the view appeared to convey little of significance to his mind, and he turned his attention back to the room itself. Along the wall opposite the fire were a dozen or so bundles of books, neatly tied with stout cord, and a dark mahogany sideboard, the left-hand door of which stood open to reveal a small collection of assorted tumblers and glasses, and an unopened bottle of whiskey. Everywhere seemed remarkably clean and tidy. A small waste-paper basket stood in the shallow alcove to the left of the fire; and inside the basket was a ball of paper, which Morse picked out and smoothed gently on the top of the sideboard:

> *Mr Quinn.*
>
> *I can't do all the cleaning this afternoon because Mr Evans is off sick and I've got to get him a prescription from the doctor.*
> *So I'll call back and finish just after six if that's convenient for you.*
>
> *A Evans (Mrs)*

Morse handed the note over to Lewis, 'Interesting.'

'How long do you think he's been dead, sir?'

Morse looked down at Quinn once more and shrugged his shoulders. 'I dunno. Two or three days, I should think.'

'It's a wonder someone didn't find him earlier.'

'Ye-es. You say he just has these downstairs rooms?'

'So Mrs Jardine says. There's a young couple living upstairs usually, but she's in the John Radcliffe having a baby, and he works nights at Cowley and he's been staying with his parents in Oxford somewhere.'

'Mm.' Morse made as if to leave, but suddenly stopped. The bottom of the door had been amateurishly planed to enable it to ride over the carpet and a noticeable draught was coming beneath it, occasionally setting the low, blue gas-jets flickering fitfully into brighter yellow flames.

'Funny, isn't, Lewis? If I lived in this room I wouldn't choose the armchair immediately in line with the draught.'

'Looks as if he did, sir.'

'I wonder, Lewis. I wonder if he did.'

Colin Dexter

TEXT LEVEL WORK

Comprehension

A 1 Where did the murder victim live?

2 What does Morse smell in the '*almost empty*' sherry glass?

3 Morse finds a '*ball of paper*' in the waste-paper basket. Who had written the note?

4 Where were the young couple who usually lived upstairs?

5 How long does Morse think the man has been dead?

B 1 Lewis says, '*Knowing you, I thought you might want me to arrest the chap who found him.*'
What does this show you about Morse's theory of murder?

2 Why do you think Morse was concerned that Lewis hadn't left his '*prints all over the place*'?

3 Why does Morse come to the conclusion that, '*We hardly need a post-mortem on this one*'?

4 How does Morse deduce which chair Quinn was sitting in before he died?

C What impression do you get of the dead man from the description of his room? Quote from the extract to support your answer.

WORD LEVEL WORK

Vocabulary

Dictionary and contextual work
Use a dictionary and the context of the passage to explain the meaning of the following words:

1 beamed	7 cyanide
2 colleague	8 dilated
3 rough	9 significance
4 inordinately	10 alcove
5 depressed	11 amateurishly
6 foetal	12 fitfully

> **HINT**
>
> Look up unfamiliar words in a dictionary.

Spelling

'tion' words
Key words: sta**tion**   informa**tion**   atten**tion**   collec**tion**

1 Use these key words in sentences of your own.

2 Learn these important 'tion' words:

concentra**tion**   evalua**tion**   loca**tion**
explana**tion**   addic**tion**   diges**tion**
solu**tion**

SENTENCE LEVEL WORK

Grammar and punctuation

Regular nouns – singular and plural

Remember, most nouns in English are regular. To make them plural we add *s* to the end, eg

colleague + *s* = colleague*s*.

We add *es* to those singulars that end in a sibilant sound (*x*, *s*, *sh* or *ch*), eg

box + *es* = box*es*.

Some nouns have two very different words for the singular and the plural, eg

woman = wom*e*n.

Some nouns are the same whether they are singular or plural, eg

one deer   many deer.

Some nouns have alternative plurals, eg

one person   many people/persons.

A Copy and complete the table.

	Singular	Plural
armchair		
body		
froth		
glass		
man		
sherry		
baby		
cyanide		
wash		
information		

B Write a sentence for each plural word in the table.

TEXT LEVEL WORK

Writing

Descriptive writing

Part of a writer's job is to make it easy for the reader to 'see' the various locations in which the story is set. This is particularly important in detective stories as the 'scene of the crime' often gives important clues as to how the crime was committed and who committed it.

In *The Silent World of Nicholas Quinn*, the writer allows the reader to see where the crime has taken place through the eyes of Morse, the investigating officer. As a detective, he must be observant as a tiny detail could be the vital clue which helps him solve the crime.

Language features

What can you see?

Morse enters the room and immediately sees the various items and furniture, eg

'the electric light ...'
'the dull-orange curtains ...'
'the gas fire ...'

What should you notice?

As well as the writer giving the reader details of what is in the room, he adds descriptive detail about each item to build up a clear picture, eg

'the electric light was still turned on'
'the dull-orange curtains were drawn'
'the gas fire was burning low'.

What could Morse safely conclude about the time of the murder from these details?

Anything unusual?

In detective fiction, the 'super-sleuth' usually solves the crime by not always taking things at face value. What others accept, he or she questions.

In this story, the murder victim appears to have sat in a chair in a draught to have his sherry.

Morse immediately questions this:

'Funny isn't it Lewis? If I lived in this room I wouldn't choose the armchair immediately in line with the draught.'

Lewis just accepts that what appears to have happened, has happened:

'Looks as if he did, sir.'

Morse is not so sure:

'I wonder, Lewis. I wonder if he did.'

Writing assignment

Write a detailed description from the point of view of the investigating officer of the scene of a crime. It can be a murder or a robbery.

Do not just make a list of the things at the scene. Give details of colour, position etc. and include a description of something that the officer feels is unusual.

It beckons you.

The story so far:

Hamlet, Prince of Denmark, has returned home from his studies to attend his father's funeral and his mother's wedding! His mother, very soon after the death of Hamlet's father, marries her first husband's brother, Claudius. Hamlet is unhappy and has a feeling that his father died in suspicious circumstances. He is told by his good friend, Horatio, that a ghost, dressed like his late father has been seen on the battlements at the hour of midnight. Hamlet is determined to see and speak to the ghost. He waits on the platform with Horatio and Marcellus and, sure enough, the ghost appears.

Act 1 Scene IV. *A guard platform.*

HORATIO
It beckons you to go away with it,
As if it some impartment did desire
To you alone.

MARCELLUS
Look with what courteous action
It waves you to a more removèd ground.
But do not go with it.

HORATIO
No, by no means.

HAMLET
It will not speak. Then I will follow it.

HORATIO
Do not, my lord.

HAMLET
Why, what should be the fear?
I do not set my life at a pin's fee,
And for my soul, what can it do to that,
Being a thing immortal as itself?
It waves me forth again. I'll follow it.

HORATIO
What if it tempt you toward the flood, my lord,
Or to the dreadful summit of the cliff
That beetles o'er his base into the sea,
And there assume some other horrible form,
Which might deprive your sovereignty of reason
And draw you into madness? Think of it.
The very place puts toys of desperation,
Without more motive, into every brain
That looks so many fathoms to the sea
And hears it roar beneath.

HAMLET
It waves me still.
Go on; I'll follow thee.

MARCELLUS
You shall not go, my lord.

HAMLET
Hold off your hands.

HORATIO
Be ruled. You shall not go.

HAMLET
My fate cries out
And makes each petty artere in this body
As hardy as the Nemean lion's nerve.
Still I am called! Unhand me, gentlemen.
By heaven, I'll make a ghost of him that lets me!
I say, away! Go on. I'll follow thee.

Exit Ghost, and Hamlet.

Scene V. *The battlements.*

Enter Ghost and Hamlet.

HAMLET
Whither wilt thou lead me? Speak; I'll go no
further.

GHOST
Mark me.

HAMLET
I will.

GHOST
My hour is almost come,
When I to sulf'rous and tormenting flames
Must render up myself.

HAMLET
Alas, poor ghost.

GHOST
Pity me not, but lend thy serious hearing
To what I shall unfold.

HAMLET
Speak. I am bound to hear.

GHOST

  I am thy father's spirit,

  Doomed for a certain term to walk the night,

  And for the day confined to fast in fires,

  Till the foul crimes done in my days of nature

  Are burnt and purged away. But that I am forbid

  To tell the secrets of my prison house,

  I could a tale unfold whose lightest word

  Would harrow up thy soul, freeze thy young blood,

  Make thy two eyes like stars start from their spheres,

  Thy knotted and combinèd locks to part,

  And each particular hair to stand on end

  Like quills upon a fearful porpentine.

  But this eternal blazon must not be

  To ears of flesh and blood. List, list, O, list!

  If thou didst ever thy dear father love ...

HAMLET

  O God!

GHOST

  Revenge his foul and most unnatural murder.

HAMLET

  Murder?

GHOST

  Murder most foul, as in the best it is,

  But this most foul, strange, and unnatural.

HAMLET

  Haste me to know't, that I, with wings as swift

  As meditation or the thoughts of love,

  May sweep to my revenge.

GHOST

  I find thee apt,

  And duller shouldst thou be than the fat weed

  That roots itself in ease on Lethe wharf,

  Wouldst thou not stir in this. Now, Hamlet, hear.

  'Tis given out that, sleeping in my orchard,

  A serpent stung me. So the whole ear of Denmark

  Is by a forgèd process of my death

  Rankly abused. But know, thou noble youth,

  The serpent that did sting thy father's life

  Now wears his crown.

HAMLET

  O my prophetic soul!

  My uncle?

William Shakespeare

TEXT LEVEL WORK

Comprehension

A 1 Who wants Hamlet to '*go away with it*'?

  2 What advice do Marcellus and Horatio give Hamlet?

  3 The ghost does not want Hamlet's pity.

  a What is the first thing it wants?
  b What is the second thing it wants?

  4 How were people led to believe Hamlet's father had died?

  5 Who does the ghost say had murdered him?

B 1 Explain in your own words:

  a '*a more removèd ground*'
  b '*I do not set my life at a pin's fee.*'
  c '*I'll make a ghost of him that lets me*'.

  2 Explain in your own words why you think Marcellus and Horatio do not want Hamlet to follow the ghost.

  3 Explain in your own words what the effect would be on Hamlet if the ghost revealed '*the secrets of my prison house*'.

C If you were in Hamlet's position, would you believe the ghost and act on what it had told you? Why? Why not?

WORD LEVEL WORK

Vocabulary

Dictionary and contextual work
Use a dictionary and the context of the passage to explain the meaning of the following words:

1	beckons	7	unfold
2	courteous	8	confined
3	immortal	9	purged
4	summit	10	revenge
5	assume	11	meditation
6	unhand	12	forged

Spelling

'ea' saying 'ee'
Key words: sp**ea**k **rea**son s**ea** **ea**se

  1 Use these key words in sentences of your own.

  2 Learn these important 'ea' words:

ben**ea**th l**ea**gue m**ea**nwhile
p**ea**ce **ea**sel dis**ea**se

SENTENCE LEVEL WORK

Grammar and punctuation

Adjectives – single words

Remember. Adjectives modify nouns. They are used to make the meaning more clear.

Adjectives also reveal more about the features of the noun, eg

intelligent whales, **aggressive** whales.

Adjectives may come in front of the noun that they modify, eg the **distressed** ghost.

These are known as *attributive adjectives*.

Adjectives may come after a linking verb, eg

The boy was **cold**.

These are known as *predicative adjectives*.

> **HINT**
>
> Adjectives are 'describing' words

A Copy and complete the table by ticking the appropriate box.

Line	Text	Attributive	Predicative
4	what courteous action		
5	removèd ground		
13	a thing immortal		
16	dreadful summit		
31	petty artere		
40	sulf'rous and tormenting flames		
50	I am forbid		
55	knotted and combinèd locks		
57	fearful porpentine		
70	apt and duller shouldst thou be		

TEXT LEVEL WORK

Writing

Persuasion

Very often in detective fiction, a character has to persuade the police of his or her innocence, and a police officer has to persuade a senior officer that they have enough evidence to arrest the guilty party.

In this scene from Hamlet, the Ghost has to persuade Hamlet that he was murdered by his brother because he wants revenge.

Language features

Layout

As this is a playscript, the conventions of layout need to be followed:

- brief description of the scene, ie '*A guard platform*'
- character's name, eg '*Horatio*'
- what the character has to say, eg '*No, by no means*'
- no direct speech punctuation.

Emotive language

The Ghost would not have been very persuasive if he had come along and said to Hamlet:

> *Ghost.* Look, your uncle murdered me. Do something about it.

The ghost uses powerful language so that Hamlet is horrified at what he is hearing:

- the ghost of his father is '*doomed ... to walk the night*'
- it is '*confined to fast in fires*'
- '*could a tale unfold whose lightest word
  Would harrow up thy soul ...*'.

The ghost plays on Hamlet's feelings of horror and sympathy to get him in the right state of mind to do what he wants.

The facts of the case

After persuading Hamlet to listen to him by playing on his emotions, the ghost states the facts very clearly:

> '*'Tis given out that, sleeping in my orchard,
> A serpent stung me ...
> But know, thou noble youth,
> The serpent that did sting thy father's life
> Now wears his crown.*'

Writing assignment

Imagine you are Hamlet shortly after the encounter with the ghost. You decide this is a police matter and make an appointment to see a Detective Inspector whom you want to investigate your father's murder.

Write a play scene between Hamlet and the Inspector where Hamlet explains what has happened.

- Is the Inspector going to believe Hamlet?
- How can Hamlet persuade the Inspector that what he is relating actually happened?

They had a house.

They had a house of crystal pillars on the planet Mars by the edge of an empty sea, and every morning you could see Mrs K eating the golden fruits that grew from the crystal walls, or cleaning the house with handfuls of magnetic dust which, taking all dirt with it, blew away on the hot wind. Afternoons, when the fossil sea was warm and motionless, and the wine trees stood stiff in the yard, and the little distant Martian bone town was all enclosed, and no one drifted out their doors, you could see Mr K himself in his room, reading from a metal book with raised hieroglyphs over which he brushed his hand, as one might play a harp. And from the book, as his fingers stroked, a voice sang, a soft ancient voice, which told tales of when the sea was red steam on the shore and ancient men had carried clouds of metal insects and electric spiders into battle.

Mr and Mrs K had lived by the dead sea for twenty years, and their ancestors had lived in the same house, which turned and followed the sun, flower-like, for ten centuries.

Mr and Mrs K were not old. They had the fair, brownish skin of the true Martian, the yellow coin eyes, the soft musical voices. Once they had liked painting pictures with chemical fire, swimming in the canals in the seasons when the wine trees filled them with green liquors, and talking into the dawn together by the blue phosphorous portraits in the speaking-room.

They were not happy now.

This morning Mrs K stood between the pillars, listening to the desert sands heat, melt into yellow wax, and seemingly run on the horizon.

Something was going to happen.

She waited.

She watched the blue sky of Mars as if it might at any moment grip in on itself, contract, and expel a shining miracle down upon the sand.

Nothing happened.

Tired of waiting, she walked through the misting pillars. A gentle rain sprang from the fluted pillar-tops, cooling the scorched air, falling gently on her. On hot days it was like walking in a creek. The floors of the house glittered with cool streams. In the distance she heard her husband playing his book steadily, his fingers never tired of the old songs. Quietly she wished he might one day again spend as much time holding and touching her like a little harp as he did his incredible books.

But no. She shook her head, an imperceptible, forgiving shrug. Her eyelids closed softly down upon her golden eyes. Marriage made people old and familiar, while still young.

She lay back in a chair that moved to take shape even as she moved. She closed her eyes tightly and nervously.

The dream occurred.

Her brown fingers trembled, came up, grasped at the air. A moment later she sat up, startled, gasping.

She glanced about swiftly, as if expecting someone there before her. She seemed disappointed; the space between the pillars was empty.

Her husband appeared in a triangular door. 'Did you call?' he asked irritably.

'No!' she cried.

'I thought I heard you cry out.'

'Did I? I was almost asleep and had a dream!'

'In the daytime? You don't often do that.'

She sat as if struck in the face by the dream. 'How strange, how very strange,' she murmured. 'The dream.'

'Oh?' He evidently wished to return to his book.

'I dreamed about a man.'

'A man?'

'A tall man, six foot one inch tall.'

'How absurd; a giant, a misshapen giant.'

'Somehow' – she tried the words – 'he looked all right. In spite of being tall. And he had – oh, I know you'll think it silly – he had *blue* eyes!'

'Blue eyes! Gods!' cried Mr K. 'What'll you dream next? I suppose he had *black* hair?'

'How did you *guess*?' She was excited.

'I picked the most unlikely colour,' he replied coldly.

'Well black it was!' she cried. 'And he had a very white skin; oh, he was *most* unusual! He was dressed in a strange uniform and he came down out of the sky and spoke pleasantly to me.' She smiled.

'Out of the sky; what nonsense!'

'He came in a metal thing that glittered in the sun,' she remembered. She closed her eyes to shape it again. 'I dreamed there was the sky and something sparkled like a coin thrown into the air, and suddenly it grew large and fell down softly to land, a long silver craft, round and alien. And a door opened in the side of the silver object and this tall man stepped out.'

'If you worked harder you wouldn't have these silly dreams.'

'I rather enjoyed it,' she replied, lying back. 'I never suspected myself of such an imagination. Black hair, blue eyes, and white skin! What a strange man, and yet – quite handsome.'

'Wishful thinking.'

'You're unkind. I didn't think him up on purpose; he just came in my mind while I drowsed. It wasn't like a dream. It was so unexpected and different. He looked at me and he said, "I've come from the third planet in my ship. My name is Nathaniel York –"'

'A stupid name; it's no name at all,' objected the husband.

'Of course it's stupid, because it's a dream,' she explained softly. 'And he said, "This is the first trip across space. There are only two of us in our ship, myself and my friend Bert."'

'*Another* stupid name.'

'And he said, "We're from a city on *Earth*; that's the name of our planet,"' continued Mrs K. 'That's what he said. "Earth" was the name he spoke. And he used another language. Somehow I understood him. With my mind. Telepathy, I suppose.'

Mr K turned away. She stopped him with a word 'Yll?' she called quietly. 'Do you ever wonder if – well, if there *are* people living on the third planet?'

'The third planet is incapable of supporting life,' stated her husband patiently. 'Our scientists have said there's far too much oxygen in their atmosphere.'

'But wouldn't it be fascinating if there were people? And they travelled through space in some sort of ship?'

'Really, Ylla, you know how I hate this emotional wailing. Let's get on with our work.'

Ray Bradbury

TEXT LEVEL WORK

Comprehension

A 1 How does:

    a Mrs K spend her mornings?
    b Mr K spend his afternoons?

  2 How was the house '*flower-like*'?

  3 Give a detailed description of Mrs K's dream.

  4 What was the unusual visitor's name?

  5 For what reason does Mr K say that no one could live on '*the third planet*'?

B 1 Explain in your own words:

    a '*never tired of the old songs*'
    b '*Wishful thinking*'
    c '*She closed her eyes to shape it again.*'

  2 What evidence is there in the text which implies that:

    a Mrs K had had the dream before?
    b she hoped it wasn't only a dream?

  3 Explain in your own words Mr K's attitude to his wife's dream.

  4 What are your impressions of the differences in character between Mr and Mrs K? Quote to support your answer.

C What impressions do you have of:

  a the planet?
  b the Ks' house?

WORD LEVEL WORK

Vocabulary

Dictionary and contextual work

Use a dictionary and the context of the passage to explain the meaning of the following words:

1 magnetic	5 contract	9 objected
2 motionless	6 imperceptible	10 revenge
3 hieroglyphs	7 irritably	11 incapable
4 phosphorus	8 evidently	12 wailing

Spelling

'ph' saying 'f'

Key words: hierogly**phs**   **ph**os**ph**orous

  1 Use these key words in sentences of your own.

  2 Learn these important 'ph' words:

    atmos**ph**ere   **ph**ysical   apostro**ph**e   pam**ph**let

    paragra**ph**   al**ph**abet   **ph**otocopy

SENTENCE LEVEL WORK

Grammar and punctuation

Adjectival clauses

> Remember. A complex sentence is made up of an *independent clause*, which can make sense by itself, and a *dependent clause*, eg
>
> (Marriage made people old and familiar,) (while still young.)
>
> (independent clause which can stand alone and make sense) (dependent clause which must be attached to the independent clause to make sense)
>
> There are three kinds of dependent clauses:
>
> - adjective clauses
> - adverb clauses
> - noun clauses.
>
> The *adjective clause* is used to give information about a noun or a pronoun. It will begin with a relative pronoun ('who', 'whose', 'whom', 'which' and 'that') or a subordinate conjunction ('when' and 'where'). The subject is often separated from its verb by the dependent clause, eg
>
> (Mrs. K, / *Subject*) (who was very sensitive, / *dependent adjective clause*) (waited for something to happen. / *verb*)

A Copy the sentences and underline, colour or highlight the adjectival clauses:

1 Mrs K cleaned the house with handfuls of magnetic dust, which blew away on the hot wind.
2 Mr K read from a metal book that he brushed with his hand.
3 From the book a voice sang, which told tales of when the sea was red steam.
4 Once, they had liked to swim in the canals, when the wine trees filled them with green liquors.
5 In the distance, she heard her husband, who never tired of playing his book.
6 Marriage made people old and familiar, while still young.

TEXT LEVEL WORK

Writing

Dominant impression

> Successful writing allows the reader to 'see' the characters and understand their feelings. It gives the reader a clear picture of the setting and sets the 'tone' of the story. This is the dominant impression. In the beginning of the extract from *The Martian Chronicles*, the dominant impression the reader gets is one of a place where nothing happens. The planet is hot and still; the characters seem trapped by routine. Mrs K's dream changes the dominant impression. Although her husband dismisses it as nonsense, there is now a feeling of energy and expectancy. The reader feels that something is going to happen.

Language features

Setting

It is always important when you are writing a story that your readers can 'see' where it takes place. When the setting comes from the writer's imagination it is even more important that it is described in detail. In *The Martian Chronicles*, the writer wants to create the dominant impression of a hot, still setting where the pace of life is slow and predictable. To do this, he uses words and phrases such as:

* *'hot wind'*
* *'warm and motionless'*
* *'no one drifted out of their doors'*.

Characters

Characters in stories need to be more than a name! They must leave an impression in the reader's mind. Mrs and Mrs K are described by the writer so we know what they look like physically:

> *'Mrs and Mrs K were not old. They had the fair, brownish skin of the true Martian, the yellow coin eyes, the soft musical voices.'*

The dominant impression of their personalities comes through what they say and what they do.

Contrast

The writer uses contrast to change the dominant impression. In the beginning, we can see this hot, slow-moving place with the two characters who were once happy but who now drift through life in a settled, rather boring routine. The change comes when we are told:

> *'Something was going to happen.'*

Mrs K's dream interrupts this routine. It is extraordinary and full of action:

> *'He came down out of the sky ...'*
> *'He came in a metal thing that glittered in the sky ...'*.

The dominant impression is now different. The reader expects something is going to happen to change the lives of Mr and Mrs K.

Writing assignment

1 Describe a setting for a story, which takes place on another planet.

2 You must decide what the dominant impression is going to be, eg

* peaceful
* dangerous
* mysterious.

3 Introduce two characters into this setting. Through physical description, what they say and what they do, let the reader gain a clear picture of their personalities. Something has to happen which changes the dominant impression, eg

* a peaceful setting is thrown into confusion
* a dangerous setting is made safe.

Personal choice

Choose one of the following assignments.

1 Continue the story of *The Martian Chronicles* where the visitors in Mrs K's dream actually arrive. How do they react to the Martians? How do Mr and Mrs K react to them?

2 Write a paragraph to say why you would, or would not, like to read the rest of this story.

Planet Earth is blue.

Ground control to Major Tom
Ground control to Major Tom
Take your protein pills
And put your helmet on

10
Ground control to Major Tom
9 - 8 - 7 - 6
Commencing countdown, engines on
5 - 4 - 3 - 2
Check ignition
1
And may God's love be with you
Lift-off

This is ground control to Major Tom
You've really made the grade
And the papers want to know
Whose shirts you wear
Now it's time to leave the capsule
If you dare

This is Major Tom to ground control
I'm stepping through the door
And I'm floating in the most peculiar way
And the stars look very different today

For here
Am I sitting in a tin can
Far above the world
Planet Earth is blue
And there's nothing I can do

Though I'm past 100,000 miles
I'm feeling very still
And I think my space ship knows
Which way to go
Tell my wife I love her very much
She knows

Ground control to Major Tom
Your circuit's dead, there's something wrong
Can you hear me Major Tom
Can you hear me Major Tom
Can you hear me Major Tom
Can you hear

Am I floating round my tin can
Far above the Moon
Planet Earth is blue
And there's nothing I can do

David Bowie

TEXT LEVEL WORK

Comprehension

A 1 The song lyrics are a conversation. Who is speaking?

2 What are the first two instructions from Ground Control?

3 What do '*the papers*' want to know?

4 How does Major Tom describe his experience when he has left the capsule?

5 What goes wrong?

B 1 What does the writer mean when he says that Major Tom has '*really made the grade*'?

2 Major Tom describes his spaceship as '*a tin can*'. What impression does this give you of his attitude to his spaceship?

3 What evidence is there that Major Tom is quite helpless in this situation?

4 What does he say that gives the impression that he doesn't think he is coming back?

C 1 Write a paragraph to explain:

  a what impression you have gained as to how Major Tom is feeling
  b why the lyric writer created that impression.

2 What evidence does the writer introduce into the lyrics to suggest that Major Tom's mission is dangerous and that something could go wrong? Quote from the lyrics in support of your answer.

WORD LEVEL WORK

Vocabulary

Dictionary and contextual work
Use a dictionary and the context of the passage to explain the meaning of the following words:

1	protein	6	planet
2	capsule	7	peculiar
3	commencing	8	helmet
4	stars	9	circuit
5	ignition	10	control

Spelling

'ei' words
Key word: prot**ei**n

1 Use the key word in a sentence of your own.

2 Learn these important 'ei' words:

h**ei**ght   rec**ei**ve   w**ei**ght   w**ei**rd

reign   **ei**ther   dec**ei**ve

SENTENCE LEVEL WORK

Grammar and punctuation

Verbs – present tense

Remember. In English, verb tenses express the time or relative time in which an action or condition takes place.

The *simple present* is used for four main purposes:

1 to express:
    a habits, eg 'I read in bed'
    b general truths, eg 'Exeter is a city'
    c repeated actions or unchanging situations, emotions and wishes, eg 'I work in Somerset'

2 to give instructions or directions, eg
  'You drive for two miles, then you turn right'

3 to express fixed arrangements, present or future, eg
  'Your lessons start at 08.30';
  'The bus leaves at 17.25'

4 to express future time, after some conjunctions ('when', 'before', 'until'), eg
  'I'll give you the money when I see you at school'.

BE CAREFUL! The simple present is not used to express actions happening now.

> **HINT**
>
> *Verbs are 'doing' or 'being' words.*

Copy and complete the table. Explain which of the four purposes is being used. The first one has been done for you.

Verbs	Explanation of purpose
This **is** ground control ...	Purpose 1 – Unchanging situation.
	The radio contact will always be
	Ground Control.
Take your protein pill ...	Purpose
Whose shirts you **wear** ...	Purpose
The stars **look** very different ...	Purpose
I **think** my space ship knows ...	Purpose
Planet Earth **is** blue ...	Purpose

TEXT LEVEL WORK

Writing

First person narrative – conversation

In the lyrics of the song *A Space Oddity* we learn what is happening through the first person:

- Ground Control gives instructions and conveys information
- Major Tom describes what he is doing and what he sees.

Language features

Conversation

The conversation in *A Space Oddity* is more like a playscript than a story:

- there are no speech marks
- there are no speech signal words such as 'he said', 'he explained' etc.

But, unlike a playscript, there are no characters' names before the speech. The layout on the page helps the reader to identify who is speaking.

Dominant impression

The dominant impression is one of calm and control. How is Major Tom feeling when he leaves the space ship? How do the people in Ground Control feel when they discover 'something's wrong'? There is nothing to indicate panic or fear.

The one impression that does come through is that Major Tom is in a situation where he can do nothing to change what is happening.

Writing assignment

Imagine you are Major Tom. You are a highly trained astronaut who does not show fear, excitement or panic but, deep inside, you do feel these things.

Write your thoughts and feelings at each stage of the mission:

- taking your pills and putting your helmet on
- lift-off
- being told that everyone on Earth thinks you 'have made the grade'
- leaving the spaceship for your space walk
- realising that something has gone wrong.

Personal choice

Choose one of the following assignments.

1. Ground Control is a group of people who are in contact with a spacecraft throughout its mission. They check that everything is going to plan, communicate with the astronaut and are responsible for the success of the mission. Write the scene from *A Space Oddity*, set out as a playscript, from the point of view of four characters from Ground Control. Everything goes well, the lift-off is successful and there is a great feeling of excitement then something goes wrong!

2. Imagine you are Major Tom's wife. Write a diary entry for the day of his mission to show your thoughts and feelings.

A long time ago.

EXT. SPACE (FX)

TITLE CARD: A long time ago in a galaxy far, far away ...
A vast sea of stars serves as the backdrop for the main title, followed by a roll-up,
which crawls into infinity.

EPISODE I: THE PHANTOM MENACE
Turmoil has engulfed the Galactic Republic. The taxation of trade routes to outlying
star systems is in dispute.

> *Hoping to resolve the matter with a blockade of deadly battleships, the greedy*
> *Trade Federation has stopped all shipping to the small planet of Naboo.*
> *While the Congress of the Republic endlessly debates this alarming chain of*
> *events, the Supreme Chancellor has secretly dispatched two Jedi Knights, the*
> *guardians of peace and justice in the galaxy to settle the conflict ...*

PAN DOWN to reveal a small space cruiser heading TOWARD CAMERA at great
speed. PAN with the cruiser as it heads toward the beautiful green planet of Naboo,
which is surrounded by hundreds of Trade Federation battleships.

INT. REPUBLIC CRUISER – COCKPIT
In the cockpit of the cruiser, the CAPTAIN and the PILOT maneuver closer to
one of the battleships.

QUI-GON: *(off-screen voice)* Captain.
The CAPTAIN turns to an unseen figure sitting behind her.

CAPTAIN: Yes, sir?

QUI-GON: *(V.O.)* Tell them we wish to board at once.

CAPTAIN: Yes, sir.

The CAPTAIN looks to her view screen, where NUTE GUNRAY, a Neimoidian
trade viceroy, waits for a reply.

CAPTAIN: *(Cont'd)* With all due respect for the Trade Federation, the
Ambassadors for the Supreme Chancellor wish to board immediately.

NUTE: Yes, yes, of course ... ahhh ... as you know, our blockade is perfectly
legal, and we'd be happy to receive the Ambassador ... Happy to.

The screen goes black. Out of the cockpit window, the sinister battleship looms
ever closer.

EXT. FEDERATION BATTLESHIP – DOCKING BAY – SPACE (FX)
The small space cruiser docks in the enormous main bay of the Federation
battleship.

INT. FEDERATION BATTLESHIP – DOCKING BAY – SPACE

A PROTOCOL DROID, TC-14, waits at the door to the docking bay.
Two WORKER DROIDS, PK-4 and EG-9 watch.

PK-4: They must be important if the Viceroy sent one of those useless protocol gearheads to greet them.

The door opens, and the Republic cruiser can be seen in the docking bay.
Two darkly robed figures are greeted by TC-14.

TC-14: I'm TC-14 at your service. This way, please.
They move off down the hallway.

EG-9: A Republic cruiser! That's trouble ... don't you think?

PK-4: I'm not made to think.

INT. FEDERATION BATTLESHIP – CONFERENCE ROOM.

A door slides open, and the two cloaked shapes are led PAST CAMERA into the formal conference room by TC-14.

TC-14: I hope your honored sirs will be most comfortable here. My master will be with you shortly.

The droid bows before OBI-WAN KENOBI and QUI-GON JINN. He backs out the door and it closes. The JEDI lower their hoods and look out a large window at the lush green planet of Naboo. QUI-GON, sixty years old, has very long white hair in a ponytail. He is tall and striking, with blue eyes. OBI-WAN is twenty-five, with very short brown hair, pale skin, and blue eyes. Several exotic, bird-like creatures SING in a cage near the door.

OBI-WAN: I have a bad feeling about this.

QUI-GON: I don't sense anything.

OBI-WAN: It's not about the mission, Master, it's something ... elsewhere ... elusive.

QUI-GON: Don't centre on your anxiety, Obi-Wan. Keep your concentration here and now where it belongs.

OBI-WAN: Master Yoda says I should be mindful of the future ...

QUI-GON: ... but not at the expense of the moment. Be mindful of the living Force, my young Padawan.

OBI-WAN: Yes, Master ... How do you think this trade viceroy will deal with the Chancellor's demands?

QUI-GON: These Federation types are cowards. The negotiations will be short.

George Lucas

TEXT LEVEL WORK

Comprehension

A 1 What is the Trade Federation using its *'deadly battleships'* for?

2 Who has the Supreme Chancellor sent as Ambassadors to settle the conflict?

3 Who has the Trade Viceroy sent to meet the Ambassadors?

4 Which of the two Ambassadors feels uneasy about the situation?

5 What does Obi-Wan think will be the outcome of the negotiations?

B 1 Explain what you think the following mean in the film script:

a Title Card

b Pan down

c Int.

d off screen

e Ext.

2 Throughout this part of the script, the scene changes several times. List the scenes.

3 What impression do you get of the character of Qui-Gon?

4 What impression do you get of the relationship between Qui-Gon and Obi-Wan?

C Obi-Wan and Qui-Gon have been sent by the Supreme Chancellor to 'persuade' the Federation to remove their battleships from around the planet Naboo. How do you think they will 'persuade' the Federation to do this?

WORD LEVEL WORK

Vocabulary

Dictionary and contextual work

Use a dictionary and the context of the passage to explain the meaning of the following words:

1 infinity	5 resolve	9 exotic
2 turmoil	6 dispatched	10 anxiety
3 engulfed	7 maneuver	11 elusive
4 dispute	8 blockade	12 negotiations

Spelling

'ic' words

Key words: republ**ic**   exot**ic**

1 Use these key words in sentences of your own.

2 Learn these important 'ic' words:

aesthet**ic**   fab**ric**   electron**ic**   athlet**ic**

tact**ic**   chromat**ic**   stat**ic**

SENTENCE LEVEL WORK

Grammar and punctuation

Verbs – imperative

> Remember. The *imperative* mood is used in issuing orders or directives.
>
> The imperative uses the infinitive of verbs, dropping the word 'to', eg
>
>   'To close' (infinitive) becomes 'close' (imperative).
>
> In the first person plural ('we'), the infinitive is preceded by 'let's' ('let us'), eg
>
>   'Let's all go fishing'.
>
> The negative imperative is formed by placing 'don't' ('do not') before the imperative form, eg
>
>   'Don't tell my dad about the joke'.
>
> The first person plural uses 'let's not' ('let us not'), eg
>
>   'Let's not be late home'.
>
> The imperative has no effect on the word order of the rest of the sentence.

A Copy and complete the table. Indicate whether each of these extracts from the script is imperative or not.

Script	Imperative – True (T) or False (F)
A Republic cruiser!	
Happy to.	
PAN DOWN	
I'm TC-14 at your service.	
Keep your concentration here and now where it belongs.	
I'm not made to think.	
Tell them we wish to board at once.	
This way, please.	
The negotiations will be short.	
They move off down the hallway.	
Don't centre on your anxiety, Obi-Wan.	
I have a bad feeling about this.	

TEXT LEVEL WORK

Writing

Screenplay

> A *screenplay* is like a playscript in that it gives characters' names, dialogue, setting and directions. It also includes directions as to what the camera films and how the film moves from scene to scene.

Language features

Dramatic dialogue

A screen writer has to think about the characters and decide:

- how they speak
- if they have an accent
- what kind of vocabulary they use
- how they speak in the particular situation they are in.

The action

What happens in a film has to be detailed in the screenplay. This includes:

- the title card. What is the first thing seen on the screen? eg
  a vast sea of stars ...
- the setting. Where is the action taking place? eg
  INT: REPUBLIC CRUISER – COCKPIT
- the movement of the camera. Exactly what is the camera shooting, from what distance and from what angle? eg
  PAN DOWN – out of the cockpit window
- details relating to the dialogue. Where are the characters when they are speaking? eg
  off-screen.

Layout

It is important for all the people working from the screenplay that they can see clearly the difference between the dialogue, setting and actions so different styles are used:

- Dialogue. This is printed in ordinary text, eg

  Tell them we wish to board at once
- Setting. This is printed in capitals, eg

  EXT. FEDERATION BATTLESHIP – DOCKING BAY
- Action. This is printed in italics, eg

  The CAPTAIN turns to an unseen figure sitting behind her.

Writing assignment

The Trade Viceroy arrives and discusses the situation with the two Jedi Knights. Continue the script in two ways:

1 The Viceroy is very worried and is eager to avoid trouble. He is willing to remove the ships which are blockading the planet but he wants something in return.

2 The Viceroy is boastful and is not willing to listen to Obi-Wan and Qui-Gon. They have to be threatening to get him to agree to remove the ships. Remember to think carefully about:

- dialogue
- instructions for the camera
- actions
- layout.

Personal choice

Choose one of the following assignments.

1 Imagine the Jedi Knights are on the return journey from Naboo and something goes wrong with their spacecraft. Think carefully about what you have learned about the characters of the two Knights and write a short scene to show what they say and do in the emergency.

2 Write a description of the Trade Viceroy that can be used in the screenplay as he arrives to discuss the situation with the Jedi Knights.

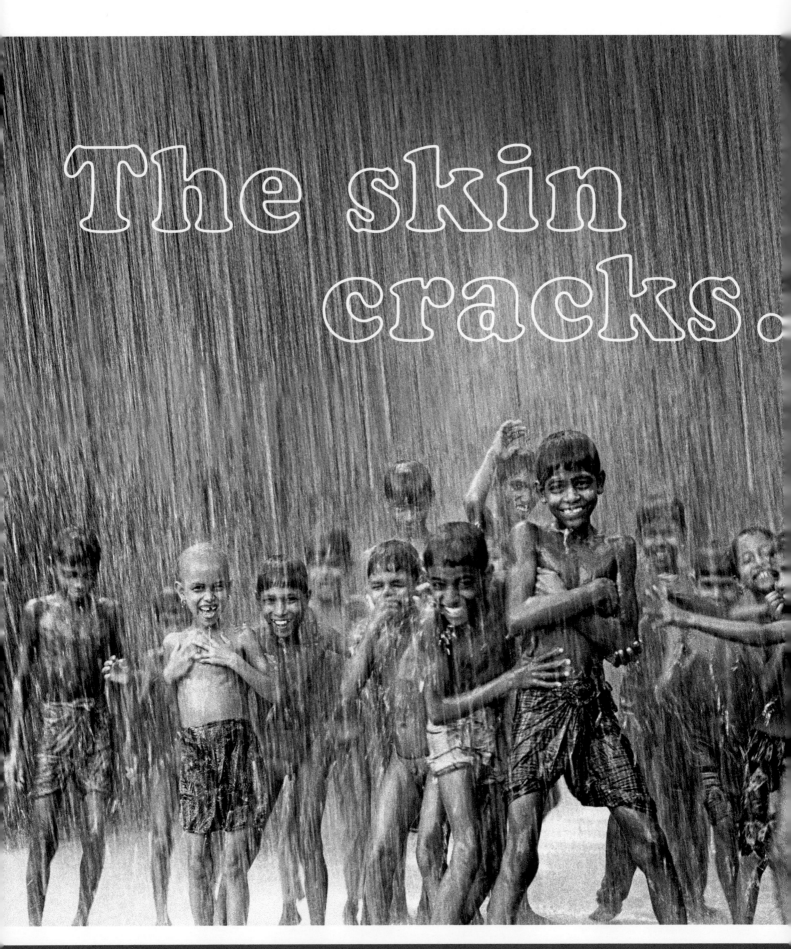

The skin cracks.

The skin cracks like a pod.
There is never enough water.

Imagine the drip of it,
the small splash, echo
in a tin mug
the voice of a kindly god.

Sometimes, the sudden rush
of fortune. The municipal pipe bursts,
silver crashes to the ground
and the flow has found
a roar of tongues. From the huts,
a congregation: every man woman
child for streets around
butts in, with pots,
brass, copper, aluminium,
plastic buckets,
frantic hands,

and naked children
screaming in the liquid sun,
their highlights polished to perfection,
flashing light,
as the blessing sings
over their small bones.

Imtiaz Dharker

Blessing – visualisation

In this passage, a Year 11 pupil, preparing for GCSE English, writes a response to a film about the poem Blessing. *The response analyses the film as a media assignment.*

The film portrays the joy brought by the arrival of water.

In the first cluster of shots the director immediately establishes the location, showing the dry environment of the slum. We see parched, cracked earth in a close-up shot to highlight the arid ground and the lack of water. A terracotta pot, noticeably the same orange/brown colour as the earth, is seen falling away from the camera and smashing dryly on the ground. As this happens the voice over begins with 'The skin ...'.

The next shot is an extreme close-up of a boy's hand falling almost lifelessly to the ground. Immediately the camera pans out to a medium close-up of the upper body of the boy lying on the ground. The sunlight in this shot is intense which again shows the scorched setting and explains why the boy is so lethargic.

The fourth shot uses a combination of sound and the sunlight to continue the theme of dryness. Another child's hand drops dirt into a metal container. As we hear the dry clink of the dirt hitting the bottom of the pot, the voice over says 'splashhh ...'. This is ironic because we expect to hear the splash of the water. Also in this shot the sunlight falls intensely through the dust falling from the child's hand.

To reach shot five, the director pans across to the right, revealing a slightly out-of-focus image of the late afternoon sun which gives it an appearance of greater intensity. In the foreground, we see another child who, although standing, wears the same exhausted, lethargic expression as the boy lying on the ground.

In the following eight or nine shots, the director introduced the water to the slum. As the voice over says 'the sudden rush of fortune ...' we see the ground split and a spray of water shoot out. Next follows a succession of medium and medium-long shots showing water all over the slum. The camera speed slows and people are caught in slow-motion running from every dwelling in the street with buckets and containers. Noticeably, there is more colour involved in this scene contrasting sharply with the dry oranges and browns of the earlier images. There are colourful clothes hanging on a washing line and people themselves appear brighter and livelier. As a background to this frenetic activity, the soundtrack produces the constant drone of excited voices.

In the final cluster of shots, we see a close-up of hands holding containers, jostling each other. The camera then pans out to reveal children dancing and playing in the water. Sunlight shines through the spray. The combination of sunlight and water highlights the contours of the children's bodies making them appear to shine. Finally, the camera zooms out slowly to show the face of the boy we saw at the beginning. He is standing, full of life, letting the water wash over his smiling face.

TEXT LEVEL WORK

Comprehension

A 1 Where does the water come from?

    2 Who comes out from the huts?

    3 What do they bring with them?

    4 What do the children do?

    5 What is the 'blessing'?

B 1 What impression does the poet create with the simile, '*The skin cracks like a pod*'?

    2 Why do you think the water is described by the metaphor as, '*the voice of a kindly god*'?

    3 When the pipe bursts, the poet says, '*silver crashes to the ground*'. In what two ways is the water like silver?

    4 What do you think the poet is describing when he uses the phrase, '*a roar of tongues*'?

C 1 Write a few sentences to explain how the poet has used contrast in the poem.

    2 The visualisation explains how a film of the poem was made. Write a paragraph to explain why you think this is, or is not, a good visual interpretation of the poem.

WORD LEVEL WORK

Vocabulary

Dictionary and contextual work

Use a dictionary and the context of the poem to explain the meaning of the following words:

1 imagine   5 congregation

2 fortune   6 frantic

3 municipal   7 perfection

4 tongues

Spelling

'er' words

Key words: wat**er**   silv**er**   copp**er**

1 Use these key words in sentences of your own.

2 Learn these important 'er' words:

        diamet**er**   perimet**er**   thermomet**er**   pref**er**

        ang**er**   numb**er**   rememb**er**

SENTENCE LEVEL WORK

Grammar and punctuation

Verbs – conditional

Remember. *Conditional verbs* are related to time. There are four different types of conditional verbs, according to the time involved.

- *Type 1*: In these sentences, the time is the present or future and the situation is real. They refer to a possible condition and its probable result. They are based on facts, and they are used to make statements about the real world, and particular situations. For example:

    'If you do not leave, I will call the manager.'

The tense in the 'if' clause is the present, and the tense in the main clause is the future.

- *Type 2*: In these sentences, the time is now or any time, and the situation is unreal. They are not based on fact, and they refer to an unlikely situation and its probable result. The use of the past tense after 'if' indicates unreality. For example:

    'If the weather was better, we would go to the beach.'

The tense in the 'if' clause is the past, and the tense in the main clause is the present conditional.

- *Type 3*: These sentences are truly hypothetical or unreal, because it is now too late for the condition or its result to exist. For example:

    'If I had known you were coming, I would have bought more food.'

The tense in the 'if' clause is the past perfect, and the tense in the main clause is the perfect conditional.

- *Type 4*: In these sentences, the time is now or always and the situation is real and possible. They are used to make statements about the real world, and often refer to general truths, such as scientific facts. For example:

    'If you freeze water, it becomes a solid.'

Both parts of the sentence are in the present tense.

TEXT LEVEL WORK

Writing

Visualisation

Many things we see on television and at the cinema began life as a book. The story, or in this case the poem *Blessing*, has to be visualised. This means that the film-makers have to translate the written word in pictures.

Language features

Organisation

The visualisation follows the storyline of the poem, ie

> **Poem**: *The skin cracks like a pod*

> **Visualisation**: *In the first cluster of shots the director immediately establishes the location, showing the dry environment of the slum.*

Each 'shot' must be clearly indicated.

The camera

You must decide:

- the distance from which the camera is shooting, eg '*in a close-up shot*'
- the angle from which the camera is shooting, eg '*from low-down, looking up*'
- the movement of the camera, eg '*camera pans left to right*'
- the speed at which the camera is shooting, eg '*the camera speed slows*'.

Attention to detail

In translating the written word into pictures, you must give precise details, eg

> '*The sunlight in this shot is intense*'

> '*... falling down steps, collecting in puddles and leaking out of pipes.*'

Sound

In the visualisation of *Blessing*, the poem is read as a voice over. The lines of the poem are matched with the visual images on the screen, eg

> *As the voice over says 'the sudden rush of fortune ...' we see the ground split and a spray of water shoot out.*

Other sounds are used as a background, eg

> *As a background to this frenetic activity, the soundtrack produces the constant drone of excited voices.*

Writing assignment

Choose a poem you particularly like, or one you have studied in class. Think carefully about how this could be visualised into a short film. Make notes on:

- how many 'shots' you will need
- which lines of the poem link with these shots
- the specific details of the poem which need to be brought out in the film
- how and where the camera will 'shoot' the film
- the background soundtrack.

Write up your notes as a visualisation of the poem.

Personal choice

Choose one of the following assignments.

1 Imagine you are the boy who we see lying on the ground at the beginning of the film. Write a first person account of the day the pipe in your village burst. Include your thoughts and feelings as well as what happened.

2 Write a poem called *Blessing* where the sun shines after a month of heavy rain and grey skies.

In the year 1866.

In the year 1866 the whole maritime population of Europe and America was excited by a mysterious and inexplicable phenomenon. This excitement was not confined to merchants, sailors, sea-captains, shippers and naval officers of all countries, but the governments of many states on two continents were deeply interested.

The excitement was caused by an enormous "something" that ships were often meeting. It was a long, spindle-shaped, and sometimes phosphorescent object, much larger and more rapid than a whale.

The different accounts that were written of this object in various log-books agreed generally as to its structure, wonderful speed, and the peculiar life with which it appeared endowed.

By taking the average of observations made at different times – rejecting the timid estimates that assigned to this object a length of 200 feet, as well as the exaggerated opinions which made it out to be a mile in width and three in length – we may fairly affirm that it surpassed all the dimensions allowed by the ichthyologists of the day, if it existed at all. It did exist, that was undeniable, and with that leaning towards the marvellous that characterises humanity, we cannot wonder at the excitement it produced in the entire world.

On the 20th of July, 1866, the steamer *Governor Higgenson*, of the Calcutta and Burnach Steam Navigation Company, met this moving mass five miles off the east coast of Australia. Captain Baker thought at first that he was in the presence of an unknown reef; he was preparing to take its exact position, when two columns of water, projected by the inexplicable object, went hissing up a hundred and fifty feet into the air. Unless there was an intermittent geyser on the reef, the *Governor Higgenson* had to do with some aquatic mammal, unknown till then, which threw out columns of water mixed with air and vapour from its blowholes.

A similar occurrence happened on the 23rd of July in the same year to the *Columbus* of the West India and Pacific Steam Navigation Company, in the Pacific Ocean. It was, therefore, evident that this extraordinary cetaceous creature could transport itself from one place to another with surprising velocity, seeing there was but an interval of three days between the two observations, separated by a distance of more than 700 nautical leagues.

Fifteen days later, two thousand leagues from the last place it was seen at, the *Helvetia*, of the Compagnie National, and the *Shannon*, of the Royal Mail Steamship Company, sailing to windward in that part of the Atlantic between the United States and Europe, each signalled the monster to each other in 42° 15' N. lat. and 60° 35' W. long. As the *Shannon* and the *Helvetia* were of smaller dimensions than the object, though they measured 300 feet over all, the minimum length of the mammal was estimated at more than 350 feet. Now the largest whales are never more than sixty yards long, if so long.

In all the great centres the monster became the fashion; it was sung about in cafés, scoffed at in the newspapers, and represented at all the theatres. It gave the opportunity for hoaxes of every description. In all newspapers short of copy imaginary beings reappeared, from the white whale, the terrible "Moby Dick" of the Northern regions, to the inordinate "Kraken", whose tentacles could fold round a vessel of 500 tons burden and drag it down to the depths of the ocean. The accounts of ancient times were reproduced: the opinions of Aristotle and Pliny, who admitted the existence of these monsters, and the Norwegian tales about Bishop Pontoppidan, those of Paul Heggede, and lastly the report of Mr Harrington, whose good faith

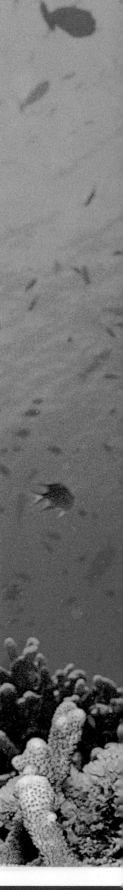

could not be put in question when he affirmed that, being on board the *Castillian*, in 1857, he saw this enormous serpent, which until then had only frequented the seas of the old *Constitutionnel* newspaper.

During the first months of the year 1867 the question seemed to be buried out of sight and mind, when fresh facts brought it again before the public. It had then changed from a scientific problem to be solved to a real and serious danger to be avoided. The questions took another phase. The monster again became an island or rock. On the 5th of March, 1867, the *Moravian*, of the Montreal Ocean Company, struck her starboard quarter on a rock which no chart gave in that point. She was then going at a rate of thirteen knots under the combined efforts of the wind and her 400 horse-power. Had it not been for the more than ordinary strength of the hull in the *Moravian* she would have been broken by the shock, and have gone down with 237 passengers.

The accident happened about daybreak. The officers on watch hurried aft, and looked at the sea with the most scrupulous attention. They saw nothing except what looked like a strong eddy, three cables' length off, as if the waves had been violently agitated. The bearings of the place were taken exactly, and the *Moravian* went on her way without apparent damage. Had she struck on a submarine rock or some enormous fragment of wreck? They could not find out, but during the examination made of the ship's bottom when under repair, it was found that part of her keel was broken.

Jules Verne

TEXT LEVEL WORK

Comprehension

A 1 Who was '*excited*' and '*deeply interested*' about the '*mysterious and inexplicable phenomenon*'?

2 What descriptive details does the writer give to help the reader 'see' the "*something*" which was causing so much excitement?

3 Who was the captain of the steamer *Governor Higgenson*?

4 How many passengers were on the *Moravian* when she was involved in an accident?

5 What damage had been done to the *Moravian*?

B 1 Explain the following in your own words:
   a '*... the monster became the fashion ...*'
   b '*... scoffed at ...*'
   c '*... frequented the seas ...*'

2 Why do you think the writer rejected '*the timid estimates*' and '*the exaggerated opinions*' when describing the '*enormous "something" that ships were often meeting*'?

3 Why does he draw the conclusion that the creature was capable of '*surprising velocity*'?

4 At what point did the existence of the 'creature' become a serious problem?

C Copy and complete the table with notes of what happened on these dates:

Date	Incident
20th July 1866	
23rd July 1866	
7th August 1866	
5th March 1867	

WORD LEVEL WORK

Vocabulary

Dictionary and contextual work

Use a dictionary and the context of the passage to explain the meaning of the following words:

1 maritime
2 inexplicable
3 endowed
4 assigned
5 affirm
6 surpassed
7 intermittent
8 cetaceous
9 velocity
10 inordinate
11 frequented
12 scrupulous

Spelling

'able' words

Key words: inexplic**able** undeni**able**

1 Use these key words in sentences of your own.

2 Learn these important 'able' words:

accept**able**   avail**able**   cap**able**   change**able**

excus**able**   irrit**able**   notice**able**

> **HINT**
>
> What do you 'notice' about **noticeable**?

SENTENCE LEVEL WORK

Grammar and punctuation

Verbs – active and passive

> Remember. There are two *voices* – active and passive – and every verb expresses one or the other. Voice connects subject and verb in a sentence by stating who carried out the action, eg
>
> The squid **attacked** the ship.
>
> 'The squid' is the subject of the active verb 'attacked', while 'the ship' is the direct object of the action.
>
> The *active* voice sentence can be changed into the *passive* voice, eg
>
> The ship **was attacked** by the squid.
>
> Grammatically, 'the ship' is now the subject of the passive verb even though it is still 'being attacked' and is the passive recipient of the squid's attack. The choice between active and passive depends on what you want to emphasise in the sentence.
>
> The passive verb form uses the auxiliary 'was', plus the past participle of the verb 'attack' ('attacked' is the past participle).

Copy and complete the table, by ticking the correct box to show whether the sentence is in the active or the passive voice.

	Active	Passive
The excitement was caused by an enormous 'something'.		
It was sung about in cafés.		
Aristotle admitted their existence.		
Mr Harrington saw an enormous serpent.		
The accident happened about daybreak.		
The Moravian was struck by something.		

TEXT LEVEL WORK

Writing

Introducing a mystery

The opening of *Twenty Thousand Leagues Under the Sea* introduces a mystery in a factual style.

It reads almost like a newspaper report of a series of incidents even though it is fiction. By using this style the writer is creating the impression of reality.

Language features

Chronology

To 'set the scene' for the mystery, the writer presents the unusual events in the order in which they happened and so builds up the suspense, eg

'*In the year 1866 ...*'

'*On the 20th of July ...*'

'*A similar occurrence happened on the 23rd of July ...*'

Description

The writer gives a detailed description of what was '*generally agreed*' about the '*something*':

'*It was a long, spindled-shaped, and sometimes phosphorescent object, much larger and more rapid than a whale.*'

Some of the description in this extract, however, is unusual because the writer is describing what people think they have seen or think they know about the '*something*'. He has to provide the reader with conflicting descriptions, eg

'*... timid estimates assigned to this object a length of 200 feet ...*'

'*... a mile in width and three in length ...*'

'*... two columns of water, projected by the inexplicable object, went hissing up a hundred and fifty feet ...*'

'*... the minimal length of the mammal was estimated at more than 350 feet.*'

Factual details

To add to the feeling of reality, the writer uses factual details which are more commonly found in non-fiction writing, eg

'*... in 42° 15' N. lat. and 60° 35' W long.*'

'*As the Shannon and the Helvetica were of smaller dimensions than the object, though they measured 300 feet over all ...*'.

Opinions

A mysterious or inexplicable occurrence will always cause debate. The writer has included the various opinions as to what the '*something*' actually was:

'*... an unknown reef ...*'

'*... an intermittent geyser ...*'

'*... some aquatic mammal ...*'

'*... the white whale, the terrible "Moby Dick"*'

'*... the inordinate "Kraken"*'

'*... enormous serpent ...*'.

Writing assignment

Write the opening paragraphs of a mystery story, following the style of *Twenty Thousand Leagues Under the Sea*:

- present a series of inexplicable but connected occurrences
- describe what people 'generally agree' that they have seen or experienced
- include factual details – times, dates, places etc – to give the introduction a feeling of reality
- recount the various opinions people have as to what it is all about.

Personal choice

Choose one of the following assignments.

1 Imagine you were a passenger aboard the *Moravian* on the 5th March, 1867. Describe what happened, your thoughts and feelings:
- before the ship struck the 'rock'
- when the ship struck the 'rock'
- when you docked and found out how serious the damage was.

2 Choose the experiences of either the *Governor Higginson* or the *Shannon* and *Helvetia* and write a front page newspaper report of the incident. Include:
- an attention-grabbing headline
- factual details of the incident
- quotes from those involved
- your own opinion, as the reporter, as to what you think occurred.

... imagine the stench.

Writers often use well-known stories and imagine what really happened. What do you think it would have been like on Noah's Ark?

They put the behemoths in the hold along with the rhinos, the hippos and the elephants. It was a sensible decision to use them as ballast; but you can imagine the stench. And there was no-one to muck out. The men were overburdened with the feeding rota, and their women, who beneath those leaping fire-tongues of scent no doubt reeked as badly as we did, were far too delicate. So if any mucking-out was to happen, we had to do it ourselves. Every few months they would winch back the thick hatch on the aft deck and let the cleaner-birds in. Well, first they had to let the smell out (and there weren't too many volunteers for winch-work); then six or eight of the less fastidious birds would flutter cautiously around the hatch for a minute or so before diving in. I can't remember what they were all called – indeed, one of those pairs no longer exists – but you know the sort I mean. You've seen hippos with their mouths open and bright little birds pecking away between their teeth like distraught dental hygienists? Picture that on a larger, messier scale. I am hardly squeamish, but even I used to shudder at the scene below decks: a row of squinting monsters being manicured in a sewer.

There was strict discipline on the Ark: that's the first point to make. It wasn't like those nursery versions in painted wood which you might have played with as a child – all happy couples peering merrily over the rail from the comfort of their well-scrubbed stalls. Don't imagine some Mediterranean cruise on which we played languorous roulette and everyone dressed for dinner; on the Ark only the penguins wore tailcoats. Remember: this was a long and dangerous voyage – dangerous even though some of the rules had been fixed in advance. Remember too that we had the whole of the animal kingdom on board: would you have put the cheetahs within springing distance of the antelope? A certain level of security was inevitable, and we accepted double-peg locks, stall inspections, a nightly curfew. But regrettably there were also punishments and isolation cells. Someone at the very top became obsessed with information gathering; and certain of the travellers agreed to act as stool pigeons. I'm sorry to report that ratting to the authorities was at times widespread. It wasn't a nature reserve, that Ark of ours; at times it was more like a prison ship.

Now, I realize that accounts differ. Your species has its much repeated version, which still charms even sceptics; while the animals have a compendium of sentimental myths. But they're not going to rock the boat, are they? Not when they've been treated as heroes, not when it's become a matter of pride that each and every one of them can proudly trace its family tree straight back to the Ark. They were chosen, they endured, they survived; it's normal for them to gloss over the awkward episodes, to have convenient lapses of memory. But I am not constrained in that way. I was never chosen. In fact, like several other species, I was specifically not chosen. I was a stowaway; I too survived; I escaped (getting off was no easier than getting on); and I have flourished. I am a little set apart from the rest of animal society, which still has its nostalgic reunions: there is even a Sealegs club for species which never once felt queasy. When I recall the Voyage, I feel no sense of obligation: gratitude puts no smear of Vaseline on my lens. My account you can trust ...

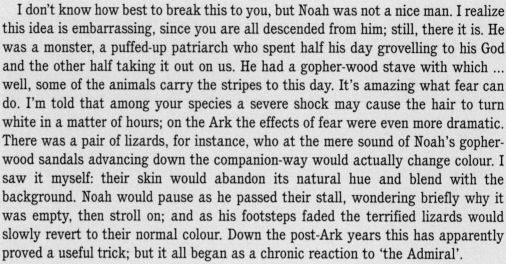

I don't know how best to break this to you, but Noah was not a nice man. I realize this idea is embarrassing, since you are all descended from him; still, there it is. He was a monster, a puffed-up patriarch who spent half his day grovelling to his God and the other half taking it out on us. He had a gopher-wood stave with which ... well, some of the animals carry the stripes to this day. It's amazing what fear can do. I'm told that among your species a severe shock may cause the hair to turn white in a matter of hours; on the Ark the effects of fear were even more dramatic. There was a pair of lizards, for instance, who at the mere sound of Noah's gopher-wood sandals advancing down the companion-way would actually change colour. I saw it myself: their skin would abandon its natural hue and blend with the background. Noah would pause as he passed their stall, wondering briefly why it was empty, then stroll on; and as his footsteps faded the terrified lizards would slowly revert to their normal colour. Down the post-Ark years this has apparently proved a useful trick; but it all began as a chronic reaction to 'the Admiral'.

Julian Barnes

TEXT LEVEL WORK

Comprehension

A 1 Why was putting the Behemoths, rhinos and hippos in the hold:
  - a sensible idea?
  - a decision which caused a problem?

2 What examples of 'security' on board the Ark does the writer give?

3 How is the 'writer' different from the other animals on board?

4 What was Noah's nickname?

5 What happened to the lizards when they heard Noah approaching?

B 1 Explain the following in your own words:
  a '*I am hardly squeamish*'
  b '*... fixed in advance ...*'
  c '*... to gloss over ...*'.

2 What impression is created by the writer when he describes the little birds as '*distraught dental hygienists*'?

3 What do you think the animals which acted as '*stool pigeons*' were doing?

4 Explain what impression the writer is trying to convey when he says, '*It wasn't a nature reserve ... it was more like a prison ship.*'

C Write a paragraph to explain how the version of Noah's Ark with which we are familiar differs from the account given in *The Stowaway*. You should consider:
  - the relationship of the animals
  - the character of Noah.

WORD LEVEL WORK

Vocabulary

Dictionary and contextual work

Use a dictionary and the context of the passage to explain the meaning of the following words:

1 behemoths	5 languorous	9 endured
2 ballast	6 inevitable	10 constrained
3 fastidious	7 curfew	11 patriarch
4 distraught	8 compendium	12 chronic

Spelling

silent 'c'

Key words: dis**c**ipline   s**c**ent   s**c**ene

1 Use these key words in sentences of your own.

2 Learn these important silent 'c' words:

dis**c**iple   s**c**ience   s**c**issors   mus**c**le

fas**c**inate   s**c**enario   s**c**hedule

SENTENCE LEVEL WORK

Grammar and punctuation

Verbs – agreement

Remember. *Singular* is 'one'.
Use 'There is' for singular nouns and collective/group nouns (one item).
Singular verbs, in the present tense, are made by adding 's'.
So, if the subject is a regular noun and DOES NOT end in 's' then the verb will end in 's', eg

The cat (no 's') meow**s** (an 's' on the verb).

When a singular collective noun has an 's', the verb STILL has an 's', eg

The class (the singular collective noun has an 's') take**s** (verb has an 's') a test.

Remember. *Plural* is 'more than one'.

Use 'There are' for plural nouns (more than one item).
When the plural noun ends in 's', the matching plural verb DOES NOT end in 's', eg

The cat**s** ('s' on noun) chase (no 's' on verb) the mice.

Even when the plural noun does not end in 's', the plural verb will still have NO 's', eg

The men (no 's' even though plural) feed (no 's' on verb) the animals.

Copy and complete the table. Choose the correct verb form from columns A or B to agree with the subject noun.

Subject noun	Verb		Sentence Remainder
	A	B	
The men	feed	feeds	the animals in the Ark.
The birds	peck	pecks	at the hippos' teeth.
The lizard	change	changes	colour when frightened.
Noah	wonder	wonders	at the empty stall.
Cleaner-birds	do	does	the mucking-out.
The big animals	was	were	ballast.

TEXT LEVEL WORK

Writing

Viewpoint

> *The Stowaway* is narrated in the first person from the point of view of the animal who has stowed away on the Ark. He expresses his opinion on the other animals, Noah and life aboard ship.

Language features

Conversational tone

The writer uses the first person and speaks directly to the reader. It is like a one-sided conversation, eg

> '... but you can imagine ...'
>
> '... but you know what I mean ...'
>
> 'Your species has its much repeated version ...'.

Writing in the first person

The writer of the story is recounting what happened, eg

> 'They put the behemoths in the hold ...'
>
> 'There was strict discipline on the Ark ...'

and how he felt, eg

> 'I am hardly squeamish ...'
>
> 'I'm sorry to report ...'.

The writer has avoided the 'trap' of beginning every sentence with 'I' which would make it boring to read, eg

> 'Now, I realise that accounts differ.'
>
> 'When I recall the voyage ...'.

Opinion

The writer is presenting his (hers/its?) opinion of life aboard the Ark and is trying to persuade readers that he is aware of why they, and the animals, would rather believe in the more popular version:

> The animals: '*But they're not going to rock the boat, are they? Not when they've been treated as heroes ...*'

People: '*Your species has its much repeated version, which still charms even the sceptics ...*'; '*... you are all descended from him ...*'.

The writer wants you to believe his version – '*My account you can trust*' – because he was there!

'*I don't know how best to break this to you ...*'.

Humour

The writer makes the account humorous through matter-of-fact observations, eg

'*... only the penguins wore tailcoats.*'

'*... there is even a Sealegs club for species which never once felt queasy.*'

'*... some of the animals carry stripes to this day ...*'.

The mysterious narrator

Just who is narrating the story? We have some clues:

'*... I was specifically not chosen. I was a stowaway ... I escaped ...*'.

What sort of animal/bird/insect do you think would not be welcome aboard the Ark?

Writing assignment

Choose a well-known story. It can be:

- a myth or legend
- a fairy story
- a story from the Bible.

Relate the story in the first person from the point of view of a human or an animal who should not have been there.
You should:

- write in a conversational tone as if you are speaking directly to the reader
- keep your own identity a mystery
- set the record straight – the popular account is not how things really happened!

Personal choice

Choose one of the following assignments.

1 Imagine you are Noah as described by the stowaway and keep a daily log book, recording what happens on the Ark. Describe one of the following incidents from your point of view:

- mucking out the hold
- punishing the animals
- pondering on why the lizards' stall always appears empty.

2 Explain why you would, or would not, like to read the rest of this story.

Relax, Mrs Jenkins.

"Alyx is a perfectly healthy child. Honestly, Martha, I don't understand why you strain so hard to come up with things to worry about!"

"Mary! How can it possibly be healthy for a six-year-old child to talk about **goblins** all the time?"

"From what you've told me, she talks about one goblin, her friend who doesn't scare her. They play follow-the-leader and hide-and-go-seek and find-the-leprechaun. It's quite normal for children to have imaginary playmates."

"A normal imaginary playmate is a child your own age who does everything you want to do. A normal imaginary playmate is **not** an eight-inch tall gray-green goblin named ... Gray-Green the Goblin!"

"So, you want your child to be creative, but not in any unusual way?"

"YES!"

Solemnly, Alyx set the cat carrier on its end in the middle of her room with the open door facing up, just like Daddy set it up when Mee-Mee needed to go to the cat-doctor. Then she spread paper and crayons out on the floor and began to draw. Soon Gray-Green's knobby, fan-eared head peeked over the sill of her room. For a few moments his big orange eyes watched the bright colors prance across the paper, then like a tumbling swirl of sticks and leaves the little creature eagerly swarmed over the sill and down beside his friend. He cuddled there contentedly and bent his head to one side with one ear unfolded upward, looking like a rather hideous cocker spaniel.

"Now I want to draw you," Alyx said, pulling over a blank sheet of paper. She patted the rug. "Stand right here so I see you head to toes."

The goblin bounced up to pose. And the little girl reached out, grabbed his ankles, hauled him upside down and dropped him head-first into the cat-carrier, slamming the door shut and flipping the latch. Then she plumped down beside him and gazed mournfully through the plastic grating at his puzzled face.

"I'm sorry, Gray-Green!" she wailed. "But Mommy says I have to keep my imagination under control!"

Several minutes later Gray-Green understood that this was not a new game and Alyx had no intention of letting him out of the carrier. He could let himself out with no problem, of course, but that wouldn't solve what he perceived as the basic problem.

Alyx ran outside to distract herself by a game of Hit Something With a Ball. Gray-Green began rocking the cat-carrier back and forth until it fell horizontally and he was no longer upside down (Alyx having forgotten this detail of what Daddy did with Mee-Mee.) The goblin continued rocking back and forth until slowly, awkward as its shape was, the carrier rolled underneath Alyx's bed. He then bided his time, making plans.

It was a day, and a night, and Alyx went off to the place called School, before Gray-Green heard the sound of the vacuum motor. He peered through the grating until two decorously shod feet approached the bed and the head of the vacuum was shoved under it. As it was pulled back for another pass, he rolled the carrier out to lay by the decorous toes, the viewing side facing upward. His claws clung to the grating and his grin stretched back to show snaggled teeth as overlarge for his head as his ears and his glowing orange eyes.

Mrs. Jenkins shrieked, dropped the handle of the vacuum cleaner, and ran. Gray-Green burst from the carrier and loped after the screaming woman, pacing himself. Just before she reached the bedside table in the Big Bedroom, he scrabbled up the right-hand wall to drop in front of the phone, still grinning. She doubled back into the Little Room beside Alyx's room. Before he let her pass through there he had a merry time scuttering around miscellaneous piles of Things Put Out of the Way, knocking them into her way, or posing on top of them to grin at her. He did let her out of there into the dining room, where she headed straight through the living room toward the front door. He let her get within a yard or so before leaping to the ceiling, spidering across it, and dropping to hang by his hindclaws from the top sill of the door, grinning upside down. She turned back to head through the dining room to the kitchen phone. Her screams were beginning to get hoarse, and this time, although he scrabbled up the arch between the dining room and kitchen, he let her pass through just before he swiped his claws down past her hair. That extra bit of teasing meant he had to bound to get onto the wall beside the kitchen phone just in time to make her pull her reaching hand back as from a hot stove. She turned to the back door, but he was in front of it. Stumbling now and gasping for air, she headed to her last refuge, the laundry room. He hung back to let her reach it. He relaxed in the doorway, leaning against the lintel and gazing up where she huddled on top of the dryer and underneath the cabinets, peering between her knees, her housedress tangled around her legs and her arms pulling them tightly to her chest.

"Relax, Mrs. Jenkins," the goblin purred. "I'm just your imagination." His grin spread wider than ever, showing off all his over-sized teeth. "All you have to do is ... control me."

Anitra L Freeman

TEXT LEVEL WORK

Comprehension

A 1 Is Alyx a boy or a girl?

2 What is the name of Alyx's cat?

3 What is the name of Alyx's mother?

4 How old is Alyx?

5 Which three games does Alyx play with her friend?

B 1 Explain why Alyx's mother is worried.

2 Explain how Alyx tricked Gray-Green, in order to capture it.

3 Describe what Gray-Green looks like.

4 What impression do you get of Gray-Green's character, from the way it behaves towards Alyx's mother? Quote from the story to support your answer.

C 1 The writer gives the impression that Gray-Green is quick enough and clever enough to manipulate Alyx's mother. Find and copy two examples where the writer describes Gray-Green's:

a physical movements

b control of Alyx's mother.

2 How does the writer create an impression of the fear that Alyx's mother feels, once she encounters Gray-Green? Quote from the story in support of your views.

WORD LEVEL WORK

Vocabulary

Dictionary and contextual work

Use a dictionary and the context of the passage to explain the meaning of the following words:

1 leprechaun	4 solemnly	7 hideous	10 shod
2 goblin	5 sill	8 mournfully	11 loped
3 creative	6 prance	9 decorous	12 miscellaneous

Spelling

'ea' saying short 'e'

Key words: h**ea**lthy   spr**ea**d   m**ea**nt

1 Use these key words in sentences of your own.

2 Learn these important 'ea' words:

j**ea**lous   w**ea**lth   w**ea**ther   spr**ea**dsheet   m**ea**sure   h**ea**vy

SENTENCE LEVEL WORK

Grammar and punctuation

Adverbial clauses

Remember, a clause is a part of a sentence that contains both a subject and a verb. A main clause can be a sentence all by itself; it can stand alone. A subordinate clause cannot stand alone, it needs a main clause to complete the sentence.

A *simple sentence* is made up of one main clause, eg

'*Alyx is a perfectly healthy child.*'

A *compound sentence* is two or more simple sentences, joined by a conjunction, eg

'*He peered through the grating until two decorously shod feet approached the bed and the head of the vacuum was shoved under it.*'

A *complex sentence* is one main clause and one or more other clauses, called subordinate clauses, eg

'*A normal imaginary playmate is a child your own age* (main clause) *who does everything you want to do* (subordinate clause).'

One type of subordinate clause is an *adverbial clause*.
Adverbial clauses tell us something about the sentence's main verb:
when, why and under what conditions the action was done, eg

    Alyx trapped Gray-Green   after tricking him by drawing.

        Main clause   Subordinate clause

Adverbial clauses may begin with a *conjunction*, which shows that
the action depends on what happened before: words like, 'when',
'if' and 'although'.

A Write out these sentences, underlining the subordinate adverbial clauses.

1 When Mrs. Jenkins was hoovering, she saw Gray-Green.

2 Although Alyx was creative, Mrs. Jenkins worried about her.

3 Gray-Green terrified Mrs. Jenkins, because he was a goblin.

4 Mrs. Jenkins cowered on top of the dryer when she was cornered by the goblin.

5 If Mrs. Jenkins had believed in goblins, Gray-Green would have been friendly.

B Copy and complete the exercise below by filling in the conjunctions that make up
the adverbial clauses. Use the **best** words from the list provided but use each
word only once.

whenever	and	after	before	during	until
because	furthermore	consequently	indeed		

1 Alyx spread paper and crayons on the floor _____ began to draw.

2 Alyx pretended to be absorbed in her drawing _____ grabbing Gray-Green
by the ankles.

3 Gray-Green rocked the trap backwards and forwards _____ it fell over.

4 Gray-Green terrorised Mrs. Jenkins _____ she did not believe in him.

5 _____ Alyx trapped him, Gray-Green was determined to get his own
back on Mrs. Jenkins.

TEXT LEVEL WORK

Writing

Dialogue

Many stories include conversation: this is called *dialogue*.
In *Just Imagine*, the writer begins the story with a section of dialogue
to set up the plot situation, ie Mrs. Jenkins is worried about Alyx.
There is a brief example of dialogue, in the middle of the story.
The story also ends with dialogue.

Mrs. Jenkins and her friend, discuss 'back and forth', giving the
reader information on the situation. The speaking characters are
'developed' through the dialogue – we learn that Mrs. Jenkins is
an anxious person. Also, the dialogue has a theme – what is real
and what is imaginary?

Language features

Dialogue gives the reader information about a character's:

- personality • occupation • nationality • social position or social class.

Dialogue also:

- advances the action by referring to the main conflict and shows conversational give and take.

Punctuating dialogue

1 Write each person's spoken words, as a separate paragraph eg

> *"So, you want your child to be creative, but not in any unusual way?"*
> *"YES!"*

2 Closely related narrative can be included within the same paragraph as the dialogue eg

> *"Now I want to draw you," Alyx said, pulling over a blank sheet of paper. She patted the rug. "Stand right here so I see you head to toes."*

3 When one person's speech continues for more than one paragraph, use speech marks to begin the speech and at the beginning – but not the end – of each new paragraph. To end the speech, use speech marks.

4 When writing continuous prose, use punctuation to introduce or to conclude a speech eg

> *"Relax, Mrs. Jenkins," the goblin purred. "I'm just your imagination."*

5 Put commas and full stops inside final speech marks eg

> *"All you have to do is ... control me."*

Natural language:

- **Use of language:** use dialogue that sounds like ordinary speech.
- **Dialogue:** helps the scene to progress and develops a better understanding of the characters.
- **Exposition:** avoids the characters explaining the plot or repeating information for the audience.
- **Overuse of particular words:** vary the use of words like 'said', eg 'shouted', 'exclaimed', 'cried', 'whispered', 'stammered'.

Writing assignment

Imagine that you are Gray-Green, the goblin, listening to:

- Mr. Jenkins, arriving home to be confronted by his distressed wife
- Mrs. Jenkins trying to convince her husband to deal with the goblin.

Using the information above, write the dialogue that Gray-Green would hear. Give the reader information about Mr. Jenkins' character and the situation.

Check that you have punctuated the dialogue correctly.

Personal choice

Choose one of the following assignments.

1 Write an extension to the story, describing how Mr. and Mrs. Jenkins deal with the situation, involving Alyx and Gray-Green.

2 Write an extension to the story, from the point of view of Alyx and Gray-Green and how they deal with Mr. and Mrs. Jenkins' attempts to solve the problem of the 'goblin'.

The sun was sinking.

The Fellowship of the Ring is the first of three books in The Lord of the Rings. *The Lord of the Rings is Sauron, the Dark Lord, who long ago lost the One Ring of power and wishes to reclaim it. The ring falls into the hands of Frodo Baggins, a hobbit. The wizard Gandalf persuades Frodo to set out with three of his hobbit friends to keep the ring out of Sauron's hands. They are hunted by the nine Ringwraiths, servants of Sauron, but, with the help of a man named Aragorn, they reach safety in Rivendell. Frodo accepts the task of taking the ring to the Cracks of Doom to destroy it. A group, known as the Fellowship is gathered to help Frodo. The Fellowship sets out through Moria, the ancient kingdom of the dwarves. Gandalf falls into the chasm of Khazad-dum while protecting the company from the Balrog, a terrifying, demonic monster. The rest of the Fellowship journeys on to Lorien, the home of the elves.*

The sun was sinking behind the mountains, and the shadows were deepening in the woods, when they went on again. Their paths now went into thickets where the dusk had already gathered. Night came beneath the trees as they walked, and the Elves uncovered their silver lamps.

Suddenly they came out into the open again and found themselves under a pale evening sky pricked by a few early stars. There was a wide treeless space before them, running in a great circle and bending away on either hand. Beyond it was a deep fosse lost in soft shadow, but the grass upon its brink was green, as if it glowed still in memory of the sun that had gone. Upon the further side there rose to a great height a green wall encircling a green hill thronged with mallorn-trees taller than any they had yet seen in all the land. Their height could not be guessed, but they stood up in the twilight like living towers. In their many-tiered branches and amid their ever-moving leaves countless lights were gleaming, green and gold and silver. Haldir turned towards the Company.

'Welcome to Caras Galadhon!' he said. 'Here is the city of the Galadhrim where dwell the Lord Celeborn and Galadriel the Lady of Lórien. But we cannot enter here, for the gates do not look northward. We must go round to the southern side, and the way is not short, for the city is great.'

There was a road paved with white stone running on the outer brink of the fosse. Along this they went westward, with the city ever climbing up like a green cloud upon their left; and as the night deepened more lights sprang forth, until all the hill seemed afire with stars. They came at last to a white bridge, and crossing found the great gates of the city: they faced south-west, set between the ends of the encircling wall that here overlapped, and they were tall and strong, and hung with many lamps.

Haldir knocked and spoke, and the gates opened soundlessly; but of guards Frodo could see no sign. The travellers passed within, and the gates shut behind them. They were in a deep lane between the ends of the wall, and passing quickly through it they entered the City of the Trees. No folk could they see, nor hear any feet upon the paths; but there were many voices, about them, and in the air above. Far away up on the hill they could hear the sound of singing falling from on high like soft rain upon the leaves.

They went along many paths and climbed many stairs, until they came to the high places and saw before them amid a wide lawn a fountain shimmering. It was lit by silver lamps that swung from the boughs of trees, and it fell into a basin of silver, from which a white stream spilled. Upon the south side of the lawn there stood the mightiest of all the trees;

its great smooth bole gleamed like grey silk, and up it towered, until its first branches, far above, opened their huge limbs under shadowy clouds of leaves. Beside it a broad white ladder stood, and at its foot three Elves were seated. They sprang up as the travellers approached, and Frodo saw that they were tall and clad in grey mail, and from their shoulders hung long white cloaks.

'Here dwell Celeborn and Galadriel,' said Haldir. 'It is their wish that you should ascend and speak with them.'

One of the Elf-wardens then blew a clear note on a small horn, and it was answered three times from far above. 'I will go first,' said Haldir. 'Let Frodo come next and with him Legolas. The others may follow as they wish. It is a long climb for those that are not accustomed to such stairs, but you may rest upon the way.'

As he climbed slowly up Frodo passed many nets: some on one side, some on another, and some set about the bole of the tree, so that the ladder passed through them. At a great height above the ground he came to a wide *talan*, like the deck of a great ship. On it was built a house, so large that almost it would have served for a hall of Men upon the earth. He entered behind Haldir, and found that he was in a chamber of oval shape, in the midst of which grew the trunk of the great mallorn, now tapering towards its crown, and yet making still a pillar of wide girth.

The chamber was filled with a soft light; its walls were green and silver and its roof of gold. Many Elves were seated there. On two chairs beneath the bole of the tree and canopied by a living bough there sat, side by side, Celeborn and Galadriel. They stood up to greet their guests, after the manner of Elves, even those who were accounted mighty kings. Very tall they were, and the Lady no less tall than the Lord; and they were grave and beautiful. They were clad wholly in white; and the hair of the Lady was of deep gold, and the hair of the Lord Celeborn was of silver long and bright; but no sign of age was upon them, unless it were in the depths of their eyes; for these were keen as lances in the starlight, and yet profound, the wells of deep memory.

Haldir led Frodo before them, and the Lord welcomed him in his own tongue. The Lady Galadriel said no word but looked long upon his face.

'Sit now beside my chair, Frodo of the Shire!' said Celeborn. 'When all have come we will speak together.'

Each of the companions he greeted courteously by name as they entered. 'Welcome Aragorn son of Arathorn!' he said. 'It is eight and thirty years of the world outside since you came to this land; and those years lie heavy on you. But the end is near, for good or ill. Here lay aside your burden for a while!'

'Welcome son of Thranduil! Too seldom do my kindred journey hither from the North.'

'Welcome Gimli son of Glóin! It is long indeed since we saw one of Durin's folk in Caras Galadhon. But today we have broken our long law. May it be a sign that though the world is now dark better days are at hand, and that friendship shall be renewed between our peoples.' Gimli bowed low.

J R R Tolkien

TEXT LEVEL WORK

Comprehension

A 1 What is the name of the city in which the travellers find themselves?

2 What is the name of the tall trees which encircle the city?

3 Which two elves rule the city?

4 Where does Frodo come from?

5 Who was Aragorn's father?

B 1 Explain what the elf rulers look like. Quote from the passage to support your answer.

2 What impressions do you get of the city? Refer to details from the passage to support your answer.

3 Explain the following in your own words:

a 'clad in grey mail'
b 'a wide talan'
c 'a pillar of wide girth'.

4 Explain what you think the elf king means when he says, 'May it be a sign that though the world is now dark better days are at hand'.

C 1 The writer has created a fantasy world, with some real and some imaginary features. Find and copy two examples of:

a language that sounds old-fashioned
b physical details that are old.

2 Explain why you think the writer goes to great lengths to stress the lineage and history of the characters, their family and their connections with the elves.

WORD LEVEL WORK

Vocabulary

Dictionary and contextual work

Use a dictionary and the context of the passage to explain the meaning of the following words:

1 tuckets	5 thronged	9 shimmering
2 dusk	6 twilight	10 bole
3 fosse	7 canopied	11 boughs
4 brink	8 grave	12 kindred

Spelling

'ow' words

Key words: shad**ow** gl**ow**ed **ow**n foll**ow** b**ow**ed

1 Use these key words in sentences of your own.

2 Learn these important 'ow' words:

arr**ow**	bel**ow**	holl**ow**	mead**ow**
sl**ow**	thr**ow**	tomorr**ow**	

SENTENCE LEVEL WORK

Grammar and punctuation

Complex sentences

> Remember. A *simple sentence* is made up of one main clause eg
>
> '*Gimli bowed low.*'
>
> A *complex sentence* is made up of one main clause and one or more other clauses, called *subordinate clauses*. A subordinate clause cannot stand alone, it needs a main clause to complete the sentence eg
>
> The others may follow as they wish.
>
> Main clause   Subordinate clause

A Copy these complex sentences and underline the main clause in each one.

1 *The Fellowship of the Ring* is the first of three books in *The Lord of the Rings.*
2 Frodo accepts the task of taking the ring to the Cracks of Doom to destroy it.
3 Haldir led Frodo before them, and the Lord welcomed him in his own tongue.
4 The Lady Galadriel said no word but looked long upon his face.
5 'When all have come we will speak together.'

TEXT LEVEL WORK

Writing

Description

> Good description helps the reader to imagine the setting for a story, atmosphere surrounding the characters and the events taking place. Good description uses key elements to create vivid impressions and to make characters and actions come alive.
>
> Descriptive writing needs:
>
> - fresh and varied vocabulary
> - unusual comparisons
> - descriptions of sight, sound, smell, taste and touch or qualities, eg 'beautiful', 'delicate'.

Language features

Setting

In order for a reader to gain the right impression and to create a living image of the setting for the events, the writer needs to give details of:

1 *the places* in which the action happens eg

'*in the woods*'
'*open wide treeless space*'
'*road paved with white stone*'
'*amid a wide lawn a fountain shimmering*'

2 *the times* at which events take place, and in which period (past, present, future) eg

'*evening sky*'
'*night came*'.

Mood

Writers also try to establish moods surrounding the characters and events, by giving details of *feelings* of harshness, sadness, or other emotions, eg

'*soft shadow*'
'*grave and beautiful*'.

Clues to the progress of events

Writers try to prepare the reader for events that will take place, eg

'*"Here dwell Celeborn and Galadriel," said Haldir. "It is their wish that you should ascend and speak with them."*'

An overall or dominant impression

Most writers wish the reader to gain a particular impression of characters or events. They want the reader to sympathise with a character, or to see that a situation is tragic, through careful description and word choices, eg

'*Each of the companions he greeted courteously*'.

A dominant impression is created using language that refers to the senses – sight, sound, smell, taste, touch or other qualities, eg

- colour – '*there rose to a great height a green wall encircling a green hill*'; '*basin of silver*'; '*white stream spilled*'; '*clad in grey mail*'
- light or dark – '*gleamed like grey silk*'; '*the hair of the Lord Celeborn was of silver long and bright*'
- sound – '*the sound of singing*'; '*clear note on a small horn*'.

Figurative language

Descriptive language often reaches its most powerful form in the images known as *figurative language*, such as:

- *Metaphor* (a comparison suggesting that something is something else) eg '*shadowy clouds of leaves*'; '*wells of deep memory*'; '*afire with stars*'
- *Simile* (a comparison using 'like' or 'as') eg '*like the deck of a great ship*'; '*like living towers*'; '*keen as lances*'
- *Personification* (giving inanimate objects, or ideas, the behaviours or qualities of a living being) eg '*lights sprang forth*'; '*years lie heavy on you*'
- *Hyperbole* (exaggeration) eg '*ever-moving leaves*'; '*countless lights*'.

Writing assignment

Write an episode of a story, in which the setting, the mood and the events, change dramatically eg from peace to conflict, from calm to panic. You should consider:

- times
- places
- feelings
- events
- dominant impression
- senses
- figurative language.

Personal choice

Choose one of the following assignments.

1 Imagine that you have been abducted by unknown beings and have been taken, blindfolded, to an alien environment. Describe what you see, when the blindfold is removed.

2 Write the opening paragraphs of a story of your own, in which you are arriving at an exotic location, which you have never visited before.

TEXT LEVEL WORK

Comprehension

A 1 What is Monkeyman's real first name?

2 What is the name of Monkeyman's uncle?

3 What is the name of Monkeyman's girlfriend?

4 What type of vehicle is Monkeyman riding in?

5 What is the name of the thief who steals Monkeyman's transport?

B 1 Explain why Monkeyman's girlfriend thinks that he should not fight the thief.

2 Explain why Monkeyman is able to ignore his girlfriend's advice and is able to take over the driving of the vehicle.

3 What gives you the impression that Monkeyman's girlfriend might not know that he is 'Monkeyman'?

4 Explain the following in your own words:

    a *'giddyup'*

    b *'gotcha'*

    c *'I'm on my way home'*.

5 Explain why the writer has put the word 'WHOOSH' in the last frame. What impression is the writer trying to create?

C 1 Explain what we learn about the situation at the beginning of the comic, when Monkeyman's girlfriend says, *'Thank you for taking us to the theatre'*.

  2 Why do you think that one of the pictures shows half of the character's face as Monkeyman and half as an ordinary man?

WORD LEVEL WORK

Vocabulary

Dictionary and contextual work

Use a dictionary and the context of the extract to explain the meaning of the following words.

1 hack	4 boarded	7 collapsed	10 splendid
2 cab	5 shortcut	8 bets	11 hero
3 coppers	6 getaway	9 kid	12 escape

Spelling

Double 't' words

Key words: attack   matter

  1 Use these key words in sentences of your own.

  2 Learn these important double 't' words:

    palette   settlement   latter   chatter

    mutter   splutter   shatter

SENTENCE LEVEL WORK

Grammar and punctuation

Direct speech

Remember. When you write down exactly what someone says, you are using *direct speech*.

When we use direct speech in writing, we place the words spoken in between speech marks (sometimes called *inverted commas*) that may be either 'single' or "double", and there is no change in these words. The speech marks go around what is being said: the punctuation comes inside the inverted commas. Start a new paragraph *every* time the speaker changes.

Even though the words spoken would form a sentence on their own, they are followed by a comma (not a full stop) when the verb of saying and its subject come afterwards, eg

"I'm on my way home," Cheater said.

BUT questions and exclamations are an exception to the rule, eg

"Uncle Vanya's collapsed!" Alice exclaimed.

When the subject and verb of saying begin the sentence, they are followed by a comma, and the first word actually spoken has a capital letter, eg

Michael said, "We've been boarded."

When the 'spoken sentence' is interrupted to insert the verb of saying and its subject, one comma is needed when breaking off the speech and another immediately before continuing it. The next word within the inverted commas has a small letter, because it is continuing the spoken sentence, eg

"Michael, you mustn't resist," Alice stressed, "remember Uncle Vanya's heart condition."

Copy and punctuate these sentences correctly.

1 theres the way to escape the copper ... why not take a hack
2 giddyup lets take a shortcut and head into the countryside
3 uncle vanyas unconscious declared alice
4 ive got to stop cheater said michael before he leaves the woods
5 his doctor warned us about his heart moaned alice right all bets are off yelled michael

TEXT LEVEL WORK

Writing

Comics

Comics are sequential pieces of artwork that tell some form of story, usually with the aid of dialogue presented in speech bubbles. As in films, pictures illustrate the narrative. Unlike film, the pictures are static.

Language features

Conventions of layout

Comics use:

- speech and thought bubbles
- frames to convey the passage of time
- in the same way that films use cuts and books use paragraphs, each individual section of a comic is contained within its own frame
- extra narrative is put in a frame within the frame
- characters are exaggerated and stereotyped
- superheroes are taller than the average human (a normal person is six and a half 'heads' tall, while a comic superhero is more in the region of eight)
- villains are often ugly
- actions are made more obvious by the use of movement lines
- sounds are shown through distinct sound effects (onomatopoeia) on the page
- the same major characters in every episode, identical settings, continuous relationships.

Conventions of characterisation

- dialogue is colloquial, eg '*... all bets are off ...*'
- language is exaggerated, eg '*So, you wanna be a hero, eh, kid?*'
- speech and thought bubbles, eg '*I've got to do something ...*'
- frequent use of exclamation marks, eg '*Gotcha!*'

Issues

- stereotypical characters
- male-dominated
- over-simplified 'good vs evil' themes
- violent action is the norm
- primary colours have impact but lack subtlety.

Writing assignment

Using the information below, finish the *Monkeyman* comic story.
You should consider different narrative conclusions, eg

- a tragic ending – Uncle Vanya dies – Monkeyman is killed by Cheater
- traditional, heroic ending – Monkeyman overcomes Cheater
- comic endings – Monkeyman loses but is rescued by Alice.

You should use only 12 frames. You will need to show that you have applied the conventions of the comic strip genre.

The dialogue
Always leave room for speech bubbles.

The story
There's not room to show everything in a comic, so use narrative boxes to propel the story along.

The angle
Use odd angles and perspectives to make the frames 'jump out of the page'.

The noise
What would comics be without those enormous sound effects?

Personal choice

Choose one of the following assignments.

1 Translate the *Monkeyman* story from a comic strip into an extended prose story, including description and dialogue.

2 Write the *Monkeyman* story as a playscript, with stage directions.

Her legs buckled.

A young native American, of the Apsaalooka tribe, is determined to become a warrior but is refused by the elders. She follows a war party, seeking revenge for the death of her father at the hands of a rival tribe. Becoming lost and losing her pony, she wanders in the wilderness, struggling to survive.

In the woods she comes across the corpse of a man, who had been killed by a grizzly bear. As she is making this discovery, she looks up to see the bear, thirty paces away. Thinking its food is in danger of being taken, the bear charges ...

Her legs buckled. She fell facedown into the dirt, and tried to curl into herself to protect her guts. Almost before she hit the ground, ivory claws as long as her fingers flashed past her face, and the roar seemed to burst her ears as the bear reached over her body and slammed a paw into her shoulder.

Then there was quiet.

Could it be over so quickly? Her spirit-soul must have slipped away for a time. But she was still in her body, still alive; she smelled the dirt pressed against her face and felt pain in her arm. Was the bear still here? She dared not move, dared not even relax an eyelid to peer through.

Suddenly a low growl vibrated close to her ear. She clutched her breath inside her chest. She could feel her skin prickling and tried to smooth it with her mind. The bear's breath was foul and his saliva dripped onto her neck and ran under her chin. He shoved at her with his muzzle, but, screaming inside, she did not twitch a muscle. The bear jabbed a paw under her hip and rolled her onto her back. *Keep rolling, protect your belly*, she told herself. Everything her father had tried to teach her from the story of his battle with the she-bear rose to the surface of her mind and body. As if from the force of the bear's shove, she rolled back onto her face, coming to rest on the corpse.

She could not hold her breath much longer. Her lungs ached. Still the bear grunted and shuffled around her.

Finally the air burst from her lungs, and instantly she sucked in another gulp and held it, hoping that the heave of her ribs and the tiny rushing sound had escaped the bear's notice.

He let out a bellow and smashed a paw down on her ribs with a crack. Her hands flew to cover the back of her neck just before the bear's jaws closed around it. She screamed as the teeth pierced her hands. She wrenched one free and grasped blindly for her knife.

Seemingly confused by the thing caught in his mouth, the grizzly twisted his jaws and tried to shake her hand from his teeth. With her free hand she found the knife, and fumbled for a grip. She had it. With all her might she drove the blade into the grizzly's throat.

The bear howled with pain. Blindly, she thrust again and again. Blood spurted from the golden fur. She stabbed again and the blade broke off in his neck. The bear shook her hand loose and she jerked it back, scrambling for some other weapon as he bore down.

The girl's hand closed around something – the corpse's broken shinbone. She wrenched it free of the knee and plunged the jagged end into the bear's gaping mouth, goring the back of his throat. For an instant he stared in surprise and pain, then began choking. He sent up a wailing like all the spirits of the dead, retching and clawing at his face, trying to scrape the bone from his throat.

She tried to scramble toward a nearby pine tree, but the bear lunged after her. In another breath he would crash down on her; she could not possibly escape. Crazily, she tried to burrow into the ground. Her hands struck the corpse and she clutched at it, squirmed under it, dragging it on top of her. The maddened bear screamed and swatted the corpse with such force it knocked her breath out. Snorting and choking, he dragged and batted the body about as if it were a fish, then crushed it in his jaws.

He retched again, spraying blood, and staggered backward.

He had put some distance between them. She leaped for the lowest branch of the pine and clawed her way up. The grizzly bounded to the tree, but she had climbed beyond his grasp. She kept climbing, higher, higher, before she dared stop and cling to the slender trunk, gasping in relief.

The bear's roar seemed to shake the tree. To her horror she realized the tree *was* shaking. The beast was shoving it with his great paws. She clutched the trunk as he rammed it with his bulk. The tree lurched, ripped up at the roots. She screamed as it began to fall. It crashed against some other pines, and she grabbed at one of them and grasped it to her breast, wrapping her arms and legs around the trunk.

Her eyes clenched shut. Above her terrified whimpering she heard noises that sounded like the bear digging. She heard the scrape of his claws, a sputtering in his throat. She heard the thud of his massive body when his legs collapsed under him, and the long rasp that was his last breath.

She did not open her eyes. For a long while she did not move, only clung to the tree like a frightened child to its mother.

Finally, slowly, she let herself down the pine trunk, a little drop at a time. When her feet touched the ground her legs were trembling so violently she crumpled to the dirt.

The bear lay in a heap nearby, motionless and massive as a mountain. A slight breeze ruffled the long grizzled gold hairs on his back. Above the blood-matted fur of his chest his frothy mouth hung slightly open. His eyes stared dully.

Diane Matchek

TEXT LEVEL WORK

Comprehension

A 1 To which Indian tribe did the girl in the story belong?

2 What does the girl find in the woods?

3 What animal does the girl come across in the woods?

4 What two weapons does the girl use to fight off the animal?

5 What type of tree does the girl climb?

B 1 Explain the following in your own words:

a '*Her spirit-soul must have slipped away ...*'

b '*... grasped blindly ...*'

c '*... goring the back of his throat ...*'.

2 Explain what injuries the girl receives in the fight with the animal.

3 Which details does the writer stress to create the awesome impression of the animal in the story?

4 What impression do you get of the way the girl reacts to the death of the animal? Quote from the passage in support of your answer.

C 1 Through the eyes of the girl the writer gives us a detailed account of what had happened. Find and copy two examples of:

a physical descriptions of the movements of the animal
b descriptions of feelings, smells or sounds.

2 Why do you think that the final paragraph could be described as a contrast to the rest of the passage? Quote from the passage in support of your answer.

WORD LEVEL WORK

Vocabulary

Dictionary and contextual work
Use a dictionary and the context of the passage to explain the meaning of the following words.

1 ivory	5 muzzle	9 bellow
2 growl	6 twitch	10 retching
3 foul	7 corpse	11 sputtering
4 saliva	8 gulp	12 rasp

Spelling

'ight' words
Key words: might   frightened   slightly

1 Use these key words in sentences of your own.

2 Learn these important 'ight' words:

highlight   light   copyright   bright
plight   night   height

SENTENCE LEVEL WORK

Grammar and punctuation

Paragraphing

Remember. A *paragraph* is a group of related sentences focusing on one topic. A *topic sentence*, giving an idea of what the subject is, often begins a paragraph. The initial idea from the topic sentence is expanded, giving more detail, information or examples.

A Copy and complete the table, ticking the appropriate column to indicate the viewpoint of the sentence.

Sentence	Bear	Girl
Thinking its food is in danger of being taken, the bear charged the girl.		
Her legs buckled.		
Ivory claws as long as her fingers flashed past her face.		
A roar seemed to burst her ears.		
The bear reached over her body and slammed a paw into her shoulder.		
She smelled the dirt pressed against her face and felt pain in her arm.		
Her hands flew to cover the back of her neck just before the bear's jaws closed around it.		
He let out a bellow and smashed a paw down on her ribs with a crack.		
Screaming inside, she did not twitch a muscle.		
She wrenched one free and grasped blindly for her knife.		
The bear jabbed a paw under her hip and rolled her onto her back.		
She screamed as the teeth pierced her hands.		
She fell face down into the dirt, and tried to curl into herself to protect her guts.		
He shoved at her with his muzzle.		
She clutched her breath inside her chest.		
The bear's breath was foul and his saliva dripped onto her neck and ran under her chin.		

B Using the sentences from **A**, above, write two paragraphs. One paragraph should be based on the bear's viewpoint. The other paragraph should be based on the girl's viewpoint.

TEXT LEVEL WORK

Writing

Paragraphing – shifting viewpoints

> Writers use paragraphing to shift the viewpoint of the story from one character to another, so the reader sees the same events from different angles. *The Sacrifice* is written in the third person – 'he', 'she', 'it' – but, although we are told what the bear does, the events are recounted from the girl's point of view.

Language features

Unity

1 Begin with a *topic sentence* showing what idea the paragraph is going to deal with.
In *The Sacrifice* the second paragraph establishes a lull in the bear's attack on the girl.
The paragraph begins with a topic sentence:
  '*Then there was quiet.*'
Then sentences build up the amazement that she has survived the attack. The paragraph keeps the same focus and topic:

> '*Could it be over so quickly? Her spirit-soul must have slipped away for a time. But she was still in her body, still alive; she smelled the dirt pressed against her face and felt pain in her arm.*'

Next, the writer begins to suggest the build-up of tension felt by the girl:

> '*Was the bear still here? She dared not move, dared not even relax an eyelid to peer through.*'

2 *Consistency and coherence* of ideas and language can be created by links known as *logical bridges*, *verbal bridges* or *transitions*:

a *logical bridges* where the same idea is carried over from sentence to sentence. So, there is a logical bridge when the girl climbs a tree in an attempt to escape the bear but the animal continues its attack:

> '*The tree lurched, ripped up at the roots.*'
> '*... it began to fall.*'

b *verbal bridges* where key words or synonyms are repeated in different sentences. In this paragraph, the writer repeats the verbal bridge of the 'tree' and similar words, such as 'trunk', eg

> '*... the tree was shaking ...*'
> '*The tree lurched, ripped up at the roots ...*'

c *transition words* can connect ideas from different sentences to show time/events, eg

> '*<u>Finally</u>, slowly, she let herself down the pine trunk, a little drop at a time. <u>When</u> her feet touched the ground her legs were trembling so violently she crumpled to the dirt.*'

Writing assignment

Write a short story about a confrontation between two characters, eg

- a wolf and a cougar
- a teenage boy and girl.

Tell the story from two points of view, by writing alternate paragraphs from the different viewpoints of the characters eg

> Paragraph 1: character A.   Paragraph 2: character B.
> Paragraph 3: character A.   Paragraph 4: character B.
> Paragraph 5: conclusion.

Do not exaggerate any physical violence. You might consider a confrontation with no physical violence and no weapons such as verbal aggression, or a character being hunted or trapped and escaping. Consider whether the confrontation ends in:

- one of the characters winning over the other
- a stalemate, in which neither character wins
- one character running away, or escaping
- 'cliff-hanger', with a mysterious but unresolved ending.

Personal choice

Choose one of the following assignments.

1 Taking the role of a third-party observer, use the story from your writing assignment. Write a new story, as if you were watching: describe what each character is doing.

2 Write a short play, with two characters, in which each character alternately describes events that they have experienced. Try to reveal, gradually, that they are describing the same series of events, for example:

Both characters were present at the scene of a crime/confrontation but have now met and each is describing the event to the other – 'Guess what I saw, yesterday'. The climax of the play will come when they realise that it was the same scene that they witnessed.

In Tse'gihi.

The Navajo Night Chant
In Tse'gihi
In the house made of the dawn,
In the house made of the evening twilight,
In the house made of the dark cloud,
In the house made of the he-rain,
In the house made of the dark mist,
In the house made of the she-rain,
In the house made of pollen,
In the house made of grasshoppers,
Where the dark mist curtains the doorway,
The path to which is on the rainbow,
Where the zigzag lightning stands high on top,
Where the he-rain stands high on top,
Oh, male divinity!
With your moccasins of dark cloud, come to us.
With your leggings of dark cloud, come to us.
With your shirt of dark cloud, come to us.
With your head-dress of dark cloud, come to us.
With your mind enveloped in dark cloud, come
    to us.
With the dark thunder above you, come to us
    soaring.
With the shapen cloud at your feet, come to us
    soaring.
With the far darkness made of the dark cloud
    over your head, come to us soaring.
With the far darkness made of the he-rain over
    your head, come to us soaring.
With the far darkness made of the dark mist
    over your head, come to us soaring.
With the far darkness made of the she-rain over
    your head, come to us soaring.
With the zigzag lightning flung out on high over
    your head, come to us soaring.
With the rainbow hanging high over your head,
    come to us soaring.
With the far darkness made of the he-rain on
    the ends of your wings, come to us soaring.
With the far darkness made of the dark mist on
    the ends of your wings, come to us soaring.
With the far darkness made of the she-rain on
    the ends of your wings, come to us soaring.
With the zigzag lightning flung out on high on
    the ends of your wings, come to us soaring.

With the rainbow hanging high on the ends of
    your wings, come to us soaring.
With the near darkness made of the dark cloud,
    of the he-rain, of the dark mist and of the
    she-rain, come to us.
With the darkness of the earth, come to us.
With these I wish the foam floating on the
    flowing water over the roots of the great corn.
I have made your sacrifice.
I have prepared a smoke for you.
My feet restore for me.
My limbs restore for me.
My body restore for me.
My mind restore for me.
My voice restore for me.
Today, take out your spell for me.
Today, take away your spell for me.
Away from me you have taken it.
Far off from me, it is taken.
Far off you have done it.
Happily I recover.
Happily my interior becomes cool.
Happily my eyes regain their power.
Happily my head becomes cool.
Happily my limbs regain their power.
Happily I hear again.
Happily for me is taken off.
Happily I walk.
Impervious to pain, I walk.
Feeling light within, I walk.
With lively feelings, I walk.
Happily abundant dark clouds I desire.
Happily abundant dark mists I desire.
Happily abundant passing showers I desire.
Happily an abundance of vegetation I desire.
Happily an abundance of pollen I desire.
Happily abundant dew I desire.
Happily may fair white corn, to the ends of the
    earth, come with you.
Happily may fair yellow corn, to the ends of the
    earth, come with you.
Happily may fair blue corn, to the ends of the
    earth, come with you.
Happily may fair plants of all kinds, to the ends
    of the earth, come with you.

Happily may fair goods of all kinds, to the ends of the earth, come with you.
Happily may fair jewels of all kinds, to the ends of the earth, come with you.
With these before you, happily may they come with you.
With these behind you, happily may they come with you.
With these below you, happily may they come with you.
With these above you, happily may they come with you.
With these all around you, happily may they come with you.
Thus happily you accomplish your tasks.
Happily the old men will regard you.
Happily the old women will regard you.
Happily the young men will regard you.
Happily the young women will regard you.
Happily the boys will regard you.
Happily the girls will regard you.
Happily the children will regard you.
Happily the chiefs will regard you.
Happily, as they scatter in different directions, they will regard you.
Happily, as they approach their homes, they will regard you.
Happily may their roads back home be on the trail of pollen.
Happily may they all get back.
In beauty I walk.
With beauty before me, I walk.
With beauty behind me, I walk.
With beauty below me, I walk.
With beauty above me, I walk.
With beauty all around me, I walk.
It is finished in beauty,
It is finished in beauty,
It is finished in beauty,
It is finished in beauty.

From *Four Masterworks of American Indian Literature* edited by John Bierhorst,
University of Arizona Press. The text is the translation of Washington Matthews.

TEXT LEVEL WORK

Comprehension

A 1 Name four things that:
    a '*the house of dawn*' is made from
    b '*restore me*'.

  2 Name three things that:
    a '*I desire*'
    b '*come to us*'.

3 Name six things that '*come to us soaring*'.

4 What do '*I walk with*'?

B 1 Explain why you think that the passage is sub-titled '*The Navajo Night Chant*'.

2 Explain the following in your own words:

'*Happily I recover*'
'*... my interior becomes cool ...*'
'*... my limbs regain their power ...*'.

3 Explain why you think the Navajo would be pleased that they now feel '*impervious to pain*' and have '*light feelings*'.

4 Why do you think that the Navajo desire an abundance of:

'*vegetation*'; '*pollen*'; '*passing showers*'; '*dew*'; and '*mists*'?

C 1 Through the chant, the writer gives us a detailed account of the things that were important to a Native American's life. Find and copy two examples each of:

● clothing

● weather.

2 What do you think we learn about Native American tribal life from the emphasis that the writer places on the following section of the text?

'*Happily the old men will regard you.*
Happily the old women will regard you.
Happily the young men will regard you.
Happily the young women will regard you.
Happily the boys will regard you.
Happily the girls will regard you.
Happily the children will regard you.
Happily the chiefs will regard you.'

WORD LEVEL WORK

Vocabulary

Dictionary and contextual work
Use a dictionary and the context of the passage to explain the meaning of the following words.

1 twilight	5 moccasins	9 shapen
2 pollen	6 leggings	10 abundant
3 rainbow	7 head-dress	11 sacrifice
4 divinity	8 enveloped	12 impervious

Spelling

'oa' words
Key words: **foa**m   appr**oa**ch   r**oa**ring   r**oa**ds

1 Use these key words in sentences of your own.

2 Learn these important 'oa' words.

b**oa**t   fl**oa**t   m**oa**n   l**oa**d

s**oa**k   t**oa**st   r**oa**m

SENTENCE LEVEL WORK

Grammar and punctuation

Sentence variety

Remember. Writers change the lengths of their sentences to give variety to the rhythms of their language. The rhythms of the language help to create a mood or atmosphere. The mood reinforces the writer's attitude to the subject they are writing about, or it forms an impression in the reader that the writer wishes to create.

Poetry uses rhythm for similar purposes and line lengths can vary greatly. One technique, that helps to reveal the rhythms of a poem, is to count the syllables on each line:

- short lines will have few syllables so they will be quicker in pace
- long lines will have many syllables so they will be slower in pace
- lines with a quicker pace will usually be more up-beat/exciting/ lively etc.
- lines with a slower pace will usually be more down-beat/serious/ sad etc.

As a general guideline:

- lines with 5 syllables, or fewer, are quicker in pace
- lines with 6–10 syllables are moderate in pace
- lines with 11 syllables, or more, are slower in pace.

Copy and complete the table. Count the number of syllables in each line. Suggest whether the pace is slow (S), moderate (M) or fast (F) and what mood the line might express. The first one has been done for you.

Line	Syllables	Pace / Mood
In beauty I walk.	5	F / Joy, celebration
Feeling light within, I walk.		
In Tse'gihi		
Where the zigzag lightning stands high on top,		
With the far darkness made of the he-rain on the ends of your wings, come to us soaring.		
With your moccasins of dark cloud, come to us.		
Happily may fair blue corn, to the ends of the earth, come with you.		
Happily the young women will regard you.		
With the near darkness made of the dark cloud, of the he-rain, of the dark mist and of the she-rain, come to us.		
It is finished in beauty.		

TEXT LEVEL WORK

Writing

Poetry – repetition and imagery

> Writers use line length and repetition to give a feeling of 'movement' and rhythm to their writing. Poets use rhythm, rhyme and repetition to provide a beat and pattern for their poems.

Language features

Repetition

The Navajo Night Chant uses repetition a good deal, eg

> 'In the house made of ...'
> 'With the far darkness made of the ...'.

It also uses reversed patterns of repetition, eg

> '... restore for me.'

It even varies the patterns in other ways, eg

> 'With beauty ... , I walk.'

Imagery

Poets, in particular, make great use of imagery. They use figures of speech, or ways of saying things, so that they create impressions or 'mental pictures' in the reader/listener. These figures of speech have technical names, such as metaphor, simile, personification etc.

House of Dawn: The Navajo Night Chant uses imagery based on the environment that surrounded the Native Americans, eg

> '... dark mist curtains the doorway ...'
> '... moccasins of dark cloud ...'
> 'In beauty I walk ...'

Writing assignment

Write a poem in celebration of the natural world, such as a forest, sunset, snow or a river. You should consider:

- repetition
- rhythm and line length
- imagery.

Personal choice

Choose one of the following assignments.

1 Find a poem that you like, on the theme of the 'natural world' and write a short explanation of how the poet has used repetition, rhythm and imagery to create the desired mood.

2 Plan, write, rehearse and perform a chant of a poem about the natural world, either written by you or by someone else.

Big Eagle made sign.

The Sioux who Married the Crow Chief's Daughter

A Sioux brave, known as 'Big Eagle', is part of a war party, which comes across an isolated camp of Crow Indians. The Sioux send Big Eagle to investigate the Crow camp.

He removed his cartridge belts and knife, and placing them, along with his rifle, at the side of the tent, he at once boldly stepped inside the tepee, and going over to the man, extended his hand and shook first the man's hand, then the old woman's, and lastly the young woman's. Then he seated himself by the side of the girl, and thus they sat, no one speaking.

Finally, Big Eagle made signs to the man, explaining as well as possible by signs, that his wife had died long ago, and when he saw the girl she so strongly resembled his dead wife that he wished to marry her, and he would go back to the enemy's camp and live with them, if they would consent to the marriage of their daughter.

The old man seemed to understand, and Big Eagle again made signs to him that a party were lying in wait just a short distance from his camp. Noiselessly they brought in the horses, and taking down the tent, they at once moved off in the direction from whence they had come. The war party waited all night, and when the first rays of dawn disclosed to them the absence of the tepee, they at once concluded that Big Eagle had been discovered and killed, so they hurriedly started on their trail for home.

In the meantime, the hunting party, for this it was that Big Eagle had joined, made very good time in putting a good distance between themselves and the war party. All day they traveled, and when evening came they ascended a high hill, looking down into the valley on the other side. There stretched for two miles, along the banks of a small stream, an immense camp. The old man made signs for Big Eagle to remain with the two women where he was, until he could go to the camp and prepare them to receive an enemy into their village.

The old man rode through the camp and drew up at the largest tepee in the village. Soon Big Eagle could see men gathering around the tepee. The crowd grew larger and larger, until the whole village had assembled at the large tepee. Finally they dispersed, and catching their horses, mounted and advanced to the hill on which Big Eagle and the two women were waiting. They formed a circle around them and slowly they returned to the village, singing and riding in a circle around them.

When they arrived at the village they advanced to the large tepee, and motioned Big Eagle to the seat of honor in the tepee. In the village was a man who understood and spoke the Sioux language. He was sent for, and through him the oath of allegiance to the Crow tribe was taken by Big Eagle. This done he was presented with the girl to wife, and also with many spotted ponies.

Big Eagle lived with his wife among her people for two years, and during this time he joined in four different battles between his own people (the Sioux) and the Crow people, to whom his wife belonged.

In no battle with his own people would he carry any weapons, only a long willow coupstick, with which he struck the fallen Sioux.

At the expiration of two years he concluded to pay a visit to his own tribe, and his father-in-law, being a chief of high standing, at once had it heralded through the village that his son-in-law would visit his own people, and for them to show their good will and respect for him by bringing ponies for his son-in-law to take back to his people.

Hearing this, the herds were all driven in and all day long horses were brought to the tent of Big Eagle, and when he was ready to start on his homeward trip, twenty young men were elected to accompany him to within a safe distance of his village. The twenty young men drove the gift horses, amounting to two hundred and twenty head, to within one day's journey of the village of Big Eagle, and fearing for their safety from his people, Big Eagle sent them back to their own village.

On his arrival at his home village, they received him as one returned from the dead, as they were sure he had been killed the night he had been sent to reconnoiter the lone camp. There was great feasting and dancing in honor of his return, and the horses were distributed among the needy ones of the village.

Remaining at his home village for a year, he one day made up his mind to return to his wife's people. A great many fancy robes, dresses, war bonnets, moccasins, and a great drove of horses were given him, and his wife, and he bade farewell to his people for good, saying, "I will never return to you again, as I have decided to live the remainder of my days with my wife's people."

On his arrival at the village of the Crows, he found his father-in-law at the point of death. A few days later the old man died, and Big Eagle was appointed to fill the vacancy of chief made by the death of his father-in-law.

Subsequently he took part in battles against his own people, and in the third battle was killed on the field. Tenderly the Crow warriors bore him back to their camp, and great was the mourning in the Crow village for the brave man who always went into battle unarmed, save only the willow wand which he carried.

Thus ended the career of one of the bravest Sioux warriors who ever took the scalp of an enemy, and who for the love of his dead wife, gave up home, parents, and friends, to be killed on the field of battle by his own tribe.

Retold by Marie L McLaughlin

TEXT LEVEL WORK

Comprehension

A 1 What is the name of the Indian brave in the passage?

2 To what tribe does the brave belong?

3 What is the name of the enemy tribe?

4 How long did the brave live with his enemy, before he returned to his own tribe?

5 For how long did the brave remain with his own tribe, before he finally returned to stay with the enemy tribe?

B 1 Why do you think that the brave wished to marry a girl from an enemy tribe?

2 Why do you think that the war party hurriedly started '*on their trail for home*'?

3 Explain the following in your own words:

- '*made signs*'
- '*oath of allegiance*'
- '*a long willow coup-stick*'.

4　What do you think the writer meant when they said that twenty young men drove '*two hundred and twenty head*' from one Indian village to the other?

C 1　What impression do you get of the character of the brave, from the way the writer refers to him? Quote in support of your answer.

2　Explain why you think that the brave, who had previously refused to carry weapons against his own tribe, changed his mind after he was made chief of the enemy tribe?

WORD LEVEL WORK

Vocabulary

Dictionary and contextual work

Use a dictionary and the context of the passage to explain the meaning of the following words:

1 cartridge	5 allegiance	9 robes
2 tepee	6 coup-stick	10 war bonnets
3 resembled	7 expiration	11 moccasins
4 disclosed	8 heralded	12 scalp

Spelling

'le' words

Key words:　ri**fle**　cir**cle**　eag**le**　bat**tle**

1　Use these key words in sentences of your own.

2　Learn these important 'le' words:

　ab**le**　　tem**ple**　　peop**le**　　ang**le**

　cab**le**　　mirac**le**　　artic**le**

SENTENCE LEVEL WORK

Grammar and punctuation

Paragraphing – sequence and chronology

> Remember. A *paragraph* is a group of related sentences focusing on one topic. Paragraphs are then put into order, to make a story.
> In a sequencing paragraph, the writing describes a series of events or a process, often based on time.

1　Write a paragraph outlining how Big Eagle becomes the chief.

2　Copy and complete the table. Suggest whether the 'useful' words, in bold type, indicate order or time.

Words	Order / time
Then he seated himself by the side of the girl	
Finally, Big Eagle made signs to the man	
In the meantime, the hunting party ... made very good time in putting a good distance between themselves and the war party.	
All day they travelled	
Soon Big Eagle could see men gathering	
Finally they dispersed	
during this time	
At the expiration of two years	
On his arrival at his home village	
A few days later the old man died	
Subsequently he took part in battles	
Thus ended the career of one of the bravest of Sioux warriors	

TEXT LEVEL WORK

Writing

Paragraphing – opposing views

The writer of *The Sioux who Married the Crow Chief's Daughter* has tried to show how Big Eagle changed his loyalties from one tribe to another. Yet, despite the difficult position that he found himself in, Big Eagle managed to remain honourable, and to keep the respect of both tribes. This was an amazing achievement and illustrates what an admirable man Big Eagle must have been. The writer's admiration is expressed through the story, which is written as a third-person narrative. The paragraphs tell of the series of events that befell Big Eagle, mostly written in a time sequence.

Language features

In recounting the story of Big Eagle changing his loyalties, the writer uses different types of paragraphs:

- *Descriptive* paragraphs – write about what a person, place, or thing is like, eg paragraph 4
- *Sequencing* paragraphs – describe a series of events or a process, often based on time, eg paragraph 5
- *Explanation* paragraphs – explain how or why something happens, eg paragraph 10.

Descriptive paragraphs

In paragraph 4, the writer describes the scene of the Crow camp, when Big Eagle first sees it. The writer mentions '*a high hill*' and '*an immense camp*'. Adjectives such as 'high' and 'immense', provide descriptive detail.

Words that are useful in describing the features of a person, place or thing usually focus on the qualities of the object. They describe:

- size, colour, shape, and purpose
- location
- weight, height, length, width or speed
- comparisons of the object with the qualities of something else.

Sequencing paragraphs

In paragraph 5, the writer tells the reader of a series of events, eg '*The old man rode through ... men gathering around the tepee ... the whole village had assembled ... they dispersed ... and catching their horses, mounted and advanced to the hill ... formed a circle ... returned to the village, singing and riding in a circle ...*'

When writing about the order of events or time sequences, the following words and phrases are useful indicators for the reader:

Order

- first, second, third, etc.
- before
- then
- subsequently

- at first, initially, in the beginning
- later, after
- at last, finally

Time

- recently
- when

- previously
- afterwards, later, after

Explanation paragraphs

In paragraph 10, the writer is explaining how something happens, eg *'herds were all driven in ... horses were brought to the tent ... twenty young men were elected to accompany him ... drove the gift horses ... (to) the village of Big Eagle and fearing for their safety from his people, Big Eagle sent them back ...'*

Such explanation paragraphs usually explain the events in order but, in addition, they often draw attention to the cause of the events and the effects that arise out of those events. When writing about the causes and effects of events, useful words and phrases include:

Cause

- because
- as a result of

- since
- is due to/was due to

Effect

- therefore
- consequently
- it follows that

- thus
- hence
- if ... then

Writing assignment

Imagine that you are either Big Eagle or his bride, the Crow chief's daughter. Write your account of the events from the story, concentrating on the viewpoint of your character. Plan your paragraphs so that they:

- describe the people and places
- sequence the events in time
- explain how and why things happened as they did.

You should consider which 'useful' words and phrases you will use for the different types of paragraphs that you will write.

Personal choice

Imagine a meeting of the Sioux tribe's Council of Elders. They have heard about Big Eagle's change of loyalty and that he is coming to visit, with 220 ponies as gifts. At the meeting, two warriors speak out, Red Cloud and Crazy Horse. Red Cloud is in favour of welcoming Big Eagle *'as one returned from the dead'*. Crazy Horse believes that Big Eagle should be seized and punished for his betrayal of his own people.

Choose one of the following assignments.

1 Write the speech that Red Cloud would make, supporting Big Eagle.
2 Write the speech that Crazy Horse would make, opposing Big Eagle.

Mr Torrio is very angry.

As the lights come up the Chicago gangs are assembled in groups on the playing area, high and low. CAPONE, MAE, GUSIK (Capone's legal adviser) and ANSELMI and SCALISE (Capone's homicide squad) are standing behind CAPONE who is seated at an office table stage right. GUSIK has a table stage left with legal documents. ALL COMPANY are in suits)

EXHIBIT ELEVEN: 'THE SHARE OUT'

NEWSPANEL ... CAPONE DIVIDES CHICAGO INTO PROFIT-SHARING GANGDOMS ...

AL: Mr Torrio is very angry

SCALISE: Displeased

ANSELMI: Full of wrath

AL: Wrathful. The reason being that you bums have been knocking off each others livelihoods. Stealing from each other

O'BANION: What's he talkin'about?

ANGELO GENNA: Dat's a lie

JACOB GEISS: I ain't ever stole anything in my life

AL: (*slapping the table*) Shuddup! Dat is what you punks have been doin'. I am here to see it ceases forthwith

MAE: From now on Chicago is gonna be divided into sections

GANGSTERS: (*complain*)

AL: Listen! Each section will be the territory of one gang. You set up your own alky cooking centres and sell your bootleg in the clubs of your territory and no other

HYMIE WEISS: It's not fair

KLONDYKE MILES: I don't like it

GENNA BRUDDER: O'Banion's territory is bigger than any one else's

AL: Close 'em. Ya hear! As has been obsoived by one of Angelo's brudders – some of the aforementioned territories are bigger than what others are

MAE: So we shall share da profits

GANGSTERS: (*Uproar*)

AL: Hold it. Remember

MAE: United we flourish ...

   AL: Divided we go down da sewer

   O'BANION: Hey what are you gettin' outsa dis, Capone?

AL: I don' get nothin' outa dis, O'Banion. I merely look after your interests. I will see to it that no small time hoodlums break into your parish. Any no-count bum that tries hustling your payroll gets shovelled underground

GUSIK: For which extra service Mr Torrio and Big Al will be taking a small 10% cream off all da Chicago red light and booze takings

HYMIE WEISS: I don' like it

MAE: You don' like it. You don' join. But just remember dat if you don' belong to da organisation ...

ANSELMI: You better start locking your bedroom door at night

SCALISE: Otherwise your wife and kids will be havin' scrambled brains for breakfast

HYMIE WEISS: Upon further consideration. I think it's a very good idea

GENNA BRUDDER: Yea. It's a good idea

O'BANION: I like it

ANGELO GENNA: Sound business proposition

KLONDYKE MILES: I'm joining

JACOB GEISS: Where do I sign?

AL: Hold it Hold it! Foist let us make sure that we have established clearly each territory and its limits. Then I can protect your gang and ensure the smooth running of this beneficial syndicate. Jack Gusik, here, my legal adviser, will be takin' down the names and areas and my two ace gunners ...

SCALISE: John Scalise

AL: ... and ...

ANSELMI: Alberto Anselmi

AL: Will be ensurin' that monthly payments are made on da line wid a smile

ANSELMI: Startin' Monday week

GUSIK: Right gentlemen who is first?

(*The individual GANG LEADERS come forward and announce themselves downstage before breaking left and signing GUSIK's document*)

KLONDYKE AND MILES O'DONNELL: Klondyke and ...

MILES: Miles O'Donnell – West side Chicago and Logan Square. (*They sign with a big X*)

DION O'BANION: Dion O'Banion ...

BUGS MORAN: and Bugs Moran – The Loop district and Circulation Alley (*They leave large thumb prints as signatures*)

ANGELO GENNA: Angelo Genna. Sicilian Colony, West side on behalf of his four brudders

FIFTH BRUDDER: Five!

ANGELO GENNA: Five Brudders (*He signs by sticking a knife into the paper*)

HYMIE WEISS: Hymie Weiss – North side and Sauganash (*He signs with a little rubber stamp*)

SAM SAMOOTS AMATUNA: Sam Samoots Amatuna ...

POLACK JOE SALTIS: And Polack Joe Saltis – Near North side and Lincoln Park (*They hand in a printed address card*)

JACOB GEISS: Jacob Geiss – The Rialto ... and a few shops my life already

(*He signs with his Jewish spectacles close to the paper in great detail. The other GANGSTERS are intrigued*)

BUGS MORAN: Hey what about Spike O'Donnell and the South side?

SAM SAMOOTS AMATUNA: I believe that our colleague and trusted friend Spike O'Donnell is residing at Joliet Penitentiary at present

GANGSTERS (*laugh*)

O'BANION: (*not laughing*) Therefore he is not included in the division of territories

GANGSTERS: Agreed

AL: Thank you gentlemen. We now have real structure

MAE: You no longer require cops and lawyers. You got your own enforcement agency

GUSIK: Mr Capone is very pleased to have your co-operation, gentlemen. He will be available for private consultation here at his new address – the Four Deuces, South Wabash Avenue. You now have the freedom to put into practice any new ventures within your own city limits – but to be frank there is 'no limit' to what can be achieved in Chicago City

John Gardiner

TEXT LEVEL WORK

Comprehension

A 1 Who is Al Capone's legal adviser?

2 Which two characters are described as '*Capone's homicide squad*'?

3 In which American city is the action of the play based?

4 Where is Spike O'Donnell currently residing?

5 What is Al Capone's new address?

B 1 Explain the following in your own words:

a '*... small time hoodlums ...*'

b '*... this beneficial syndicate ...*'

c '... enforcement agency ...'
d 'Divided we go down da sewer ...'.

2 Explain what you think that the Newspanel means by 'CAPONE DIVIDES CHICAGO INTO PROFIT-SHARING GANGDOMS ...'.

3 What do you think Al Capone gets out of the arrangements he is suggesting? Quote from the script in support of your answer.

4 Explain why you think some of the characters sign the agreement with an X, by sticking a knife into the paper, with a rubber stamp, or with a thumb-print.

C 1 How does the writer try to give us the impression that these characters are tough criminals? Are they represented as clever, or not?

2 In what ways does the writer make sure that the actors communicate their backgrounds and their characters to the audience? You should consider their:

- language
- actions
- stage directions.

WORD LEVEL WORK

Vocabulary

Dictionary and contextual work
Use a dictionary and the context of the script to explain the meaning of the following words.

1 homicide	4 punks	7 obsoived	10 hoodlums
2 wrath	5 territory	8 flourish	11 consideration
3 livelihoods	6 bootleg	9 brudders	12 proposition

Spelling

Silent 't'
Key words: hustling   listen

1 Use these key words in sentences of your own.

2 Learn these important silent 't' words:

castle   fasten   often   thistle   whistle

SENTENCE LEVEL WORK

Grammar and punctuation

Standard and non-standard English

Standard English usually refers to the more formal forms (or 'registers') of the language. Much written language is formal and is in the standard English register. Spoken language is less formal and is often non-standard in its register: this is sometimes referred to as 'colloquial' or, in its cruder forms, as 'slang'.

In the playscript for *Big Al*, the language is deliberately written in non-standard register, in order to imitate the dialect of the Chicago gangsters.

Copy and complete the following table. In the space provided, underneath each non-standard sentence (NS), write your own translation into standard English (SE).

1	NS	I will see to it that no small time hoodlums break into your parish.
	SE	
2	NS	Any no-count bum that tries hustling your payroll gets shovelled underground.
	SE	
3	NS	Otherwise your wife and kids will be havin' scrambled brains for breakfast.
	SE	
4	NS	... you bums have been knocking off each others livelihoods.
	SE	
5	NS	Dat is what you punks have been doin'.
	SE	
6	NS	You set up your own alky cooking centres and sell your bootleg in the clubs ...
	SE	

TEXT LEVEL WORK

Writing

Playscripts – colloquialisms and slang

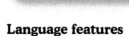

The playscript includes many words that were used in America during the 1920s and the writer has written the script so that the spelling imitates the accents of Chicago gangsters from the Irish, Italian and Jewish communities. When groups of people live together, work together, speak the same language and are interested in the same things, they often invent words or phrases to make their language special and private. At times, these groups use language which they *don't* want other people to understand – for example, servicemen, criminals and children. This sort of language is called 'slang'. Slang often becomes part of people's everyday language.

Language features

Regional variation

Slang is really a special language, in a particular place, so it changes from place to place, from group to group and over time.

When children call a truce in a game of 'Hide and seek', they use different words in different parts of the country, eg

- 'Faintes' Southern England
- 'Barley' Scotland and Wales
- 'Keys' West of Scotland and Northern England

GOSH, SIR, THAT'S THE SECOND KITE YOU'VE PRANGED THIS WEEK!

I KNOW, CURLY. I THOUGHT IT WAS CURTAINS THIS TIME!

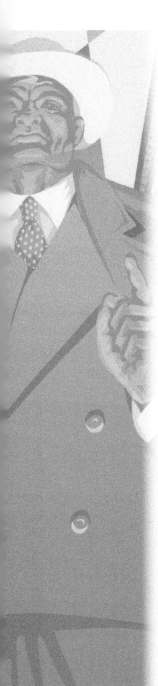

Cockney rhyming slang

A famous form of slang is Cockney rhyming slang. Phrases are used to rhyme with the standard English word, eg

- 'Whistle and flute'   suit
- 'Skin and blister'   sister
- 'North and south'   mouth
- 'Apples and pears'   stairs
- 'Mince pies'   eyes
- 'Barnet Fair'   hair
- 'Scotch pegs'   legs
- 'Tea leaf'   thief
- 'China plate'   mate
- 'Trouble and strife'   wife

Special groups

Slang is usually invented by groups of people who need to stick together. British soldiers during the two world wars, for example, invented a lot of new slang, eg

- 'Skive'   to escape duty
- 'Toe-rag'   someone who licks officers' boots
- 'Hard-case'   tough person

Foreign derivations

Some of this new slang came from travelling to countries whose languages the soldiers didn't know. During their overseas postings, soldiers often picked up words they heard but did not see written down. As a result, their use of the words was not always accurate. Examples derived from foreign languages include:

- 'Buckshee'   free (from Persian word for 'gift')
- 'Scarper'   to run away (from Italian words for 'escape')
- 'Shufti'   to have a look (from Arabic word for 'look')
- 'Blighty'   Britain (from Hindustani word for 'home')

Backslang

Children often invented secret codes of language for private talking with close friends that excluded adults, and others who did not belong to their group. These secret slangs are called *backslang*. One such backslang comes from Liverpool and is known as 'Abey Gabey', where the letters 'abey' are added in front of each vowel in a word, eg

'Babeyad labeyangabeyuage rabeyeally irrabeyitabeyates mabeye and mabeyakes mabeye crabeyoss.'

Writing assignment

Write a playscript, or a scene in which there are at least three characters, who share a slang language background. You should consider whether the slang is:

- a regional form, eg Cockney rhyming slang
- the slang of a special group, eg skate-boarders
- foreign in derivation, eg a group from other traditions or cultures
- backslang, eg Abey Gabey.

Personal choice

Choose one of the following assignments.

1 Find as many non-standard/slang words and phrases as you can and make a phrase-book, with translations into standard English.

2 Research and investigate forms of slang and non-standard language that are used amongst groups of people, in the past as well as today, eg hippies, surfers, sports groups, music groups etc.

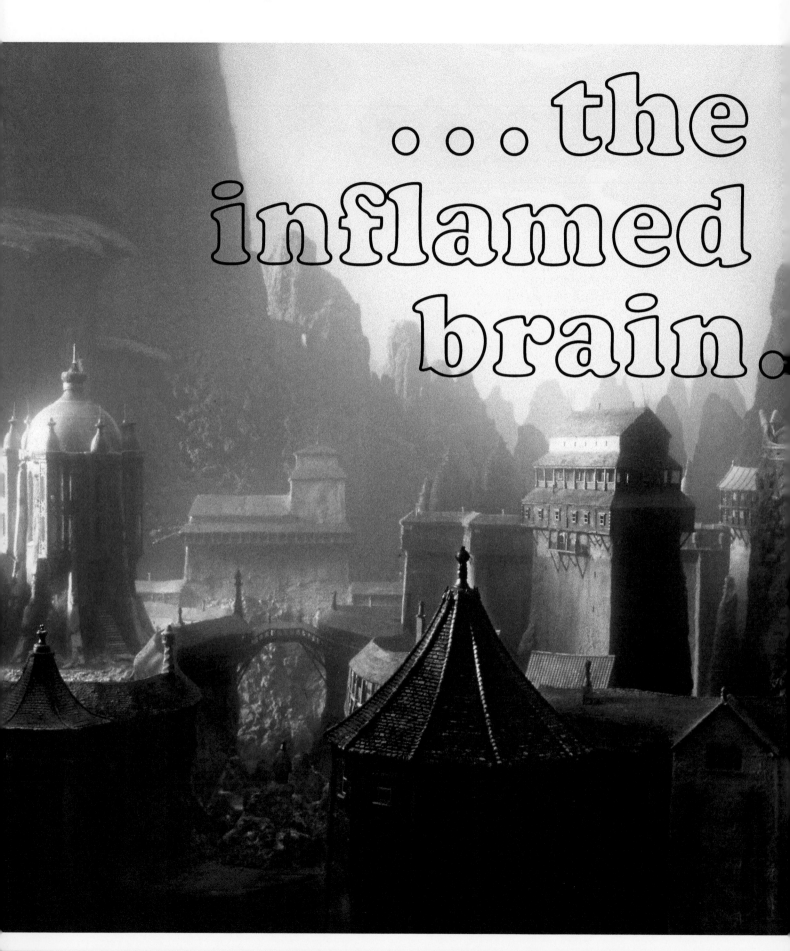

. . . the inflamed brain.

In the Gormenghast *trilogy, Mervyn Peake created an eccentric world full of dark and troublesome characters in the mad castle of Gormenghast. In the third book,* Titus Alone, *Titus 77th Earl of Groan, exiles himself from his ancestral castle, to wander in the world outside. He finds that it is just as strange and frightening as Gormenghast.*

In this extract, Titus has been trying to rescue the woman known as Black Rose but he is attacked by the villainous Veil, a 'mantis-like' figure. Cornered by Veil in a large, crowded, arena-like space, Titus is forced to fight. When Veil seems to be gaining the upper hand, help comes to Titus in the unlikely form of the melancholic Muzzlehatch.

SIXTY ONE

What is it threads the inflamed brain of the one-time killer? Fear? No, not so much as would fill the socket of a fly's eye. Remorse? He has never heard of it. It is loyalty that fills him, as he lifts his long right arm. Loyalty to the child, the long scab-legged child, who tore the wings off sparrows long ago. Loyalty to his aloneness. Loyalty to his own evil, for only through this evil has he climbed the foul stairways to the lofts of hell. Had he wished to do so, he could never have withdrawn from the conflict, for to do so would have been to have denied Satan the suzerainty of pain.

Titus had lifted his sword high in the air, and at that instant, his enemy slung his blade in the direction of the youth. It ran through the air with the speed of a stone from a sling and struck Titus's sword immediately below the handle, and sent it hurtling from his grasp.

The force of this had Titus on his back. It was as though he himself had been struck. His arms and empty hands shook and buzzed with the shock.

As he lay there he saw two things. The first thing he saw was that Veil had picked up a couple of knives from the wet ground, and was coming towards him, his neck and head craned forward, like a hen's when it runs for food, his dagger'd fists uplifted to the level of his ears. For a moment as Titus gazed spellbound the mean mouth opened and the purplish tongue sped from one corner to the other. Titus stared, all initiative, all power drained out of him, but even as he lay sprawling helplessly something moved in the tail of his eye, something above his head so that for an involuntary second he found himself staring wide-lidded at a long slippery beam, a beam that seemed to float across the semi-darkness.

But what Titus saw, and what set his pulses racing, was not the beam itself, but something that crawled along it: something massive yet absolutely silent: something that moved inexorably forward inch by inch. What it was he could not quite make out. All he could tell was that it was heavy, agile and alive.

But Mr Veil, the breaker of lives, observing how Titus had, for a fraction of a second, lifted his eyes to the shadows above, stopped for a moment his advance upon the spreadeagled youth and turned his face to the rafters. What he saw at that moment was something that brought forth from the very entrails of the vast audience, an intake of terrified breath, for the figure, huge it seemed in that wavering light, rose to its feet upon the beam, and a moment later leaped into space.

There was no computing the weight and speed of Muzzlehatch as he crushed the 'Mantis' to the slippery ground. The victim's face had been lifted so that the jaw, the clavicles, the shoulder blades and five ribs were the first to go down like dead sticks in a storm.

And yet he made no sound, this devil, this 'Mantis', this Mr. Veil. Crushed and prostrate, he rose again, and to Titus's horror it seemed as though the features of his face had all changed places.

It could also be seen that there was damage to his limbs. In trying to move away he was forced to trail a broken leg which followed him like something tied to his hip: a length of driftwood. All he could do was to hop away from Muzzlehatch with that assortment of features clustered upon his neck like a horrible nest.

But he did not go far. Titus, Muzzlehatch and the great awe-struck audience realized suddenly that the knives were still in his hands, and that his hands and arms alone had escaped the destruction. There, in his fists, they sparkled.

But he could no longer see his enemies. His face had capsized. Yet his brain had not been damaged.

'Black Rose!' he cried into the dreadful silence. 'Take your last look at me,' and he plunged the two knives through the ribs, in the region of his heart. He left them there, withdrawing his hands from the hilts.

Out of the silence that followed, the horrible sound of his laughter began to grow, and as it grew in volume, the blood poured out the quicker, until there came the moment when, with a final convulsion of his long bones, he fell upon his dislocated, meaningless face, twitched for the last time, and died.

Mervyn Peake

TEXT LEVEL WORK

Comprehension

A 1 What is the name of the 77th Earl of Groan?

2 What is the name of his castle?

3 Who is the villain seeking to destroy the 77th Earl of Groan?

4 Which character unexpectedly helps the Earl?

5 To whom does the villain cry out, just before his death?

B 1 Explain the following in your own words:

    a '... *breaker of lives ...*'
    b '... *a length of driftwood ...*'
    c '... *features clustered upon his neck ...*'.

2 Explain what you think we learn about the villain in the opening paragraphs of the passage. You should consider:

- physical appearance
- personality.

3 Explain how the villain disarms the Earl of Groan.

4 What impression do we gain of the character who saves the Earl of Groan from the villain? Quote from the passage in support of your answer.

C 1 The writer gives us a detailed account of the events that happen in the story. Find and copy two examples each of:

    a physical description of characters
    b vivid use of figurative language.

2 How, do you think, does the writer create a sense of the eccentricity and oddities of the world around the 77th Earl of Groan? Quote from the passage in support of your answer.

WORD LEVEL WORK

Vocabulary

Dictionary and contextual work

Use a dictionary and the context of the passage to explain the meaning of the following words.

1 eccentric	5 suzerainty	9 inexorably
2 exiles	6 spellbound	10 spreadeagled
3 remorse	7 initiative	11 clavicles
4 loyalty	8 involuntary	12 capsized

Spelling

'qu' words

Key words: **qu**icker   **qu**ite

1 Use these key words in sentences of your own.

2 Learn these important 'qu' words:

en**qu**ire   **qu**eue   se**qu**ence   techni**qu**e

e**qu**ation   s**qu**are   **qu**aver

SENTENCE LEVEL WORK

Grammar and punctuation

Powerful verbs

Writing is more powerful, vivid and interesting, when writers use powerful verbs. Powerful verbs are descriptive – they describe actions specifically, give more detail and create an image in the reader's mind that reflects the writer's ideas more precisely. These powerful verbs use the active voice, not passive voice eg

Active: '... his enemy slung his blade in the direction of the youth ...'
Passive: '... he was forced to trail a broken leg ...'.

By their very nature, powerful verbs are action-based and quickly suck the reader into a world of action and feeling. They also drive the reader through the text. They do this by helping to create mood and atmosphere, by generating movement and character, eg

'... the figure, huge it seemed in that **wavering** light, **rose** to its feet upon the beam, and a moment later **leaped** into space.'

Copy and complete the table. Use these powerful verbs to write a sentence of your own for each word.

Verb	Sentence
buzzed	
craned	
dagger'd	
drained	
sprawling	
wavering	
crushed	
sparkled	
capsized	
plunged	
dislocated	
twitched	

TEXT LEVEL WORK

Writing

Encounters – twists and turns

The extract from *Titus Alone* is a crisis point in the story. The writer successfully sets up a situation, which leads the reader to expect something, before building up the tension and then, unexpectedly, the narrative takes a twist.

The writer uses descriptive language and powerful verbs to create images that are vivid and engaging. Figurative language is central to this technique.

Language features

Twists and turns of the plot/situation

<u>Stage 1:</u>
The hero, Titus, engages the villain, Veil, eg

'Titus had lifted his sword high in the air ...'

<u>Stage 2:</u>
Veil easily disarms Titus, eg

'... struck Titus's sword immediately below the handle, and sent it hurtling from his grasp ...'

<u>Stage 3:</u>
It appears that our hero is going to meet an unfortunate end, at Veil's hands, eg

'Veil had picked up a couple of knives from the wet ground, and was coming towards him, his neck and head craned forward, like a hen's when it runs for food, his dagger'd fists uplifted to the level of his ears.'

Stage 4:
At that moment, an unexpected rescuer appears, eg

'... the figure, huge it seemed in that wavering light, rose to its feet upon the beam, and a moment later leaped into space ...'

Stage 5:
The villain is overthrown, eg

'There was no computing the weight and speed of Muzzlehatch as he crushed the 'Mantis' to the slippery ground.'

Stage 6:
Yet, at the last moment, the writer gives the climax another twist, as Veil survives the horrific injuries caused by Muzzlehatch, only to commit suicide, eg

'... he plunged the two knives through the ribs, in the region of his heart ...'

Figurative language
The writer uses various forms of figurative language to make the descriptions more vivid and to make comparisons.

- Metaphor:
  'What is it threads <u>the inflamed brain</u> ...'
  'No, not so much as would fill <u>the socket of a fly's eye</u>.'
  '... he climbed the foul stairways to <u>the lofts of hell ...</u>'
  '<u>dagger'd</u> fists'
  '... in <u>the tail</u> of his eye ...'
  '... beam that seemed to <u>float</u> ...'
  '... the <u>breaker of lives</u> ...'
- Simile:
  '... head craned forward, <u>like a hen's</u> when it runs for food ...'
  '... <u>like a horrible nest</u> ...'
  '... <u>like</u> something tied to his hip: <u>a length of driftwood</u> ...'
  '... <u>like dead sticks</u> in a storm ...'
- Personification:
  '... pulses <u>racing</u> ...'
- Onomatopoeia:
  '... <u>buzzed</u> with the shock ...'

Writing assignment
Write a story in stages, involving two or three main characters, just as the writer of *Titus Alone* did, in the extract. The story should have a series of twists and turns:

- set up the situation
- make the reader expect something to happen
- build up the tension
- have a twist before reaching the crisis point
- try to devise a surprise ending
- write in the 3rd person.

Personal choice
Choose one of the following assignments.

1 Plan and produce a comic strip or film storyboard for the *Titus Alone* extract. Use 12 frames in total.

2 Write a narrative poem, telling the story of the extract from *Titus Alone*. Use the six Stages above, to create six verses for the narrative poem.

3000 ducats.

In Shakespeare's play, The Merchant of Venice, *Antonio acts as a guarantor for his friend Bassanio to borrow money from Shylock, the Jew. Shylock and Antonio dislike each other. The Jew agrees to lend Bassanio the money (3,000 ducats), on condition that Antonio will give Shylock a pound of his own flesh, if they cannot repay the loan. When the time comes to repay the loan, there is a dispute between Shylock and Antonio. Eventually, the dispute comes to court, in front of the Duke, who will judge the case.*

SCENE I *Venice. A court of justice.* Enter *the* DUKE, *the* Merchants, ANTONIO, BASSANIO, GRATIANO, SALERIO, *and* Officers of the Court

DUKE

What, is Antonio here?

ANTONIO

Ready, so please your Grace.

DUKE

I am sorry for thee: thou art come to answer
A stony adversary, an inhuman wretch
Uncapable of pity, void and empty
From any dram of mercy.

ANTONIO

I have heard
Your grace hath ta'en great pains to qualify
His rigorous course; but since he stands obdurate
And that no lawful means can carry me
Out of his envy's reach, I do oppose
My patience to his fury, and am arm'd
To suffer, with a quietness of spirit,
The very tyranny and rage of his.

DUKE

Go one, and call the Jew into the court.

SALERIO

He is ready at the door: he comes, my lord.

Enter SHYLOCK

DUKE

Make room, and let him stand before our face.
Shylock, the world thinks, and I think so too,
That thou but lead'st this fashion of thy malice
To the last hour of act; and then 'tis thought
Thou'lt show thy mercy and remorse more strange
Than is thy strange apparent cruelty;
And where thou now exact'st the penalty –
Which is a pound of this poor merchant's flesh –
Thou wilt not only loose the forfeiture,
But, touch'd with human gentleness and love,
Forgive a moiety of the principal,
Glancing an eye of pity on his losses,
That have of late so huddled on his back,
Enow to press a royal merchant down,

And pluck commiseration of his state
From brassy bosoms and rough hearts of flints,
From stubborn Turks and Tartars, never train'd
To offices of tender courtesy.
We all expect a gentle answer, Jew.

SHYLOCK

I have possess'd your Grace of what I purpose;
And by our holy Sabbath have I sworn
To have the due and forfeit of my bond:
If you deny it, let the danger light
Upon your charter and your city's freedom.
You'll ask me, why I rather choose to have
A weight of carrion flesh than to receive
Three thousand ducats: I'll not answer that,
But, say, it is my humour. Is it answer'd?
What if my house be troubled with a rat,
And I be pleas'd to give ten thousand ducats
To have it ban'd? What, are you answer'd yet?
Some men there are love not a gaping pig;
Some, that are mad if they behold a cat;
And others, when the bagpipe sings i' the nose,
Cannot contain their urine: for affection,
Mistress of passion, sways it to the mood
Of what it likes or loathes.
Now, for your answer:
As there is no firm reason to be render'd,
Why he cannot abide a gaping pig;
Why he, a harmless necessary cat;
Why he, a woollen bagpipe, but of force
Must yield to such inevitable shame
As to offend, himself being offended;
So can I give no reason, nor I will not,
More than a lodg'd hate and a certain loathing
I bear Antonio, that I follow thus
A losing suit against him. Are you answer'd?

BASSANIO

This is no answer, thou unfeeling man,
To excuse the current of thy cruelty.

SHYLOCK

I am not bound to please thee with my answers.

William Shakespeare

TEXT LEVEL WORK

Comprehension

A 1 In which city does the action of the play take place?

2 Who borrows money in the play?

3 From whom is the money borrowed?

4 How much money is borrowed?

5 What forfeit is to be carried out, if the loan is not repaid on time?

B 1 Explain the following in your own words:
   a *'Your grace hath ta'en great pains to qualify his rigorous course;'*
   b *'A stony adversary'*
   c *'And pluck commiseration from his state.'*

2 Explain what you think the duke means, when he says that he *'expects a gentle answer'* from the Jew.

3 The Jew declares that the does not have what the Duke would consider good reasons for demanding the forfeit. He only says that it is his right under the law. What three 'unreasonable' examples does he refer to?

4 What impression do you get of the character of the Jew? Quote from the script in support of your answer.

C 1 Some critics claim that the play deals with 'racist' issues. Is there any evidence in the script that there are issues touching on racism?

2 What impression do you get of the relationship between the Jew and the other characters in the play? Quote from the script in support of your answer.

WORD LEVEL WORK

Vocabulary

Dictionary and contextual work
Use a dictionary and the context of the passage to explain the meanings of the following words.

1 guarantor	5 dram	9 malice
2 dispute	6 mercy	10 remorse
3 merchants	7 obdurate	11 forfeit
4 pity	8 tyranny	12 charter

Spelling

Silent 'w'
Key words: answer   wretch

1 Use these key words in sentences of your own.

2 Learn these important silent 'w' words:

playwright   wreck   wrestler   write

sword   wrong   wrap

SENTENCE LEVEL WORK

Grammar and punctuation

Shakespearean language

Shakespeare's language was different from modern English in a number of ways: vocabulary, grammar/punctuation, imagery and complexity. A modern audience can still understand Shakespeare's language, once they are used to it. Although, in *The Merchant of Venice* there are differences in issues and attitudes, there are also many similarities between Shakespeare's world and ours.

Copy and complete the table. Fill in your translation of the Shakespearean language into modern English.

Shakespearean	Modern
thou art come to answer	
hath ta'en	
he comes	
that thou but lead'st	
'tis thought	
Thou'lt show thy mercy	
exact'st the penalty	
Thou wilt not	
I be pleased	
the bagpipe sings i' the nose	
so please your grace	
Go one, and call the Jew into the court	
by our holy Sabbath I have sworn	

TEXT LEVEL WORK

Writing

Shakespeare playscript – translation

The most striking feature of Shakespeare is his command of language. Shakespeare is believed (according to the Oxford English Dictionary) to have introduced nearly 3,000 words into English. His vocabulary seems to have been about 17,000 words (four times that of a modern, well-educated English person).

Shakespeare's Elizabethan dialect differs only slightly from modern English, despite what most school pupils think. These are some differences in modern English in the use of interjections/ejaculations, the use of picturesque intensives and subject/verb/object construction.

A number of Shakespeare's words have changed their meanings or disappeared from today's vocabulary. Elizabethan word order was more flexible than today, as was their use of parallel words, such as 'thou' and 'you'. Shakespeare was also writing dramatic poetry, not standard prose, which gave rise to differences in language.

Language features

Interjections and ejaculations

The Elizabethan was likely to make greater use of words or phrases spoken out suddenly and with emphasis. These interjections or ejaculations usually add little to the content of what is being said, but are used to show the feelings of uncertainty or to assert a point, eg

'**What**, is Antonio here?'

'**What**, are you answer'd yet? '

Sentence constructions

The word order of sentences differed and was less defined in Elizabethan dialect. The subject, object and verb were sometimes structured differently compared with modern English, eg

'*Some men there are.*' We would say: 'There are some men.'

Another variation was the different order of the verb and the negative, eg

'*Love not a gaping pig.*' We would say: 'Do not love a gaping pig.'

Imaginative language

The Elizabethans, above all, loved to give their language a liveliness, intensity and flamboyance that is sometimes lost today. They would put words together in unusual combinations that created a particularly individual style, eg

'*A lodged hate.*' We would say: 'A deep-seated hate.'

'*A certain loathing.*' We would say: 'A positive disgust or detestation.'

Figurative language

Elizabethan English was focused on the language of feeling which conveyed their meaning with tremendous strength and simplicity. In order to do this, the Elizabethans made great use of figurative language, such as metaphor, simile and personification, eg

'*A stony adversary ...*'
'*Out of his envy's reach ...*'
'*... losses, That have of late so huddled on his back ...*'

Subtle differences in word use

To heighten the emotional character of a passage, Elizabethans were discriminating in their use of 'thou' and 'you'. These words could suggest different feelings in subtle ways that are not possible in modern English. 'You' was the ordinary, unemotional form which was used in ordinary speech among the educated classes. On the other hand, 'thou' could express various emotions such as anger, disgust, familiarity, superiority, or love, eg

'*I think so too, that **thou** but lead'st this fashion of thy malice*'

Here the Duke is prompting Shylock to be merciful and uses the emotionally tinged form of 'thou' to suggest a mild and friendly approach. Yet when Bassanio says, '*This is no answer, **thou** unfeeling man*', he is using 'thou' to express contempt and loathing of Shylock.

Writing assignment

Translate Shylock's main speech from the passage, into modern English. As far as you can, in your own translation, you should consider how Shakespeare used:

- interjections and ejaculations
- varied sentence constructions
- picturesque intensives
- figurative language
- emphasis on emotion in the use of 'thou'.

Personal choice

Choose one of the following assignments.

1 Imagine that you are the judge in the case of Shylock vs Antonio. Sum up the arguments that Shylock has made and give the jury guidance on how to assess the innocence or guilt of the two characters. You should consider:

- the contract that was made
- the nature of the forfeit
- the reasonableness of the demands that Shylock makes.

2 Write Bassanio's reactions to what he observes in the court, in the form of a diary. You should consider how Bassanio felt towards Antonio and Shylock and the behaviour and attitude of:

- Antonio
- Shylock
- the Duke.

Great Clarendon Street, Oxford, OX2 6DP, United Kingdom

Oxford University Press is a department of the University of Oxford.
It furthers the University's objective of excellence in research, scholarship,
and education by publishing worldwide. Oxford is a registered trade mark of
Oxford University Press in the UK and in certain other countries

First published by Nelson Thornes Ltd in 2003
This edition published by Oxford University Press in 2014

British Library Cataloguing in Publication Data
Data available

978-0-7487-6947-6

20 19 18 17 16

Printed in Great Britain by CPI Group (UK) Ltd., Croydon CR0 4YY

Acknowledgements

Illustrations: Martin Berry, Zhenya Matysiak, Peters and Zabrinsky, The Richardson Studio, and Viners Wood Associates
Page make-up: Viners Wood Associates

The authors and publishers are grateful to the following for permission to reproduce copyright material and photographs
for this book:

John Bierhorst for 'House Made of Dawn – The Navajo Night Chant' from John Bierhorst, ed, Four Masterworks of
American Indian Literature, University of Arizona Press (1984) pp. 326–30. Copyright © John Bierhorst; Bloodaxe
Books for Imtiaz Dharker, 'Blessing' from Postcards From God (1997); Bloomsbury Publishing plc for material from
Diane Matcheck, The Sacrifice (1999) pp. 78–81; Anitra Freeman for 'Just Imagine' posted on the internet 2.5.02
[anitra@spamcop.net]; Samuel French Ltd for material from John Gardiner and Andrew Parr, Big Al (1977) pp. 28–9;
HarperCollins Publishers for material from J R R Tolkien, The Lord of the Rings (1966) pp. 458–61. Copyright © 1977
J R R Tolkien; David Higham Associates on behalf of the author for material from Mervyn Peake, Titus Alone, Vintage
(1970) pp. 136–9; Lucasfilm Ltd for an illustration and text from screenplay Star Wars: Episode II – Attack of the Clones,
Ebury Press, pp. 5, 2–5. Copyright © 2002 Lucasfilm Ltd & TM; Onward Music Ltd for, 'Space Oddity', words and music by
David Bowie. Copyright © 1969, 1998 Onward Music Ltd; Pan Macmillan for material from Colin Dexter, The Silent World
of Nicholas Quinn, included in Inspector Morse Omnibus, Macmillan, London (1991) pp. 433–4, 435–7;
Abner Stein on behalf of the author for material from Ray Bradbury, 'Ylla' in The Martian Chronicles, HarperCollins
(1951) pp. 13–5; The Random House Group Ltd for material from Julian Barnes, A History of the World in 10½ Chapters,
Jonathan Cape (1989) pp. 3–4, 12; Dominic Wren for 'Blessing – visualisation'.

Carlton Television Limited, p. 10; Corel 663 (NT), p. 22; Digital Vision 7 (NT), p. 28; Digital Vision 6 (NT), p. 30;
Star Wars: Episode II – Attack of the Clones © 2002 Lucasfilm Ltd. & TM. All rights reserved. Used under authorization.
Unauthorized duplication is a violation of applicable law. p. 34; M.Rahman/UNEP/Still Pictures, p. 40; Stephen Frink/
Digital Vision LU (NT), p. 46; © Jim and Edna Cole, North Forty Creations, USA, p. 52; Photodisc 44 (NT), p. 64;
NatPhotos/Digital vision AF (NT), p. 76; Corel 12 (NT), p. 82; BBC Picture Archives, p. 100; Stockbyte 31 (NT), p. 106.

Although we have made every effort to trace and contact all copyright holders before publication this has not been
possible in all cases. If notified, the publisher will rectify any errors or omissions at the earliest opportunity.

Links to third party websites are provided by Oxford in good faith and for information only. Oxford disclaims any
responsibility for the materials contained in any third party website referenced in this work.